HENRY HUDSON
and His Voyages of Exploration in World History

Judith Edwards

Enslow Publishers, Inc.

40 Industrial Road   PO Box 38
Box 398   Aldershot
Berkeley Heights, NJ 07922   Hants GU12 6BP
USA   UK
http://www.enslow.com

Library of Congress Cataloging-in-Publication Data

Edwards, Judith, 1940-
    Henry Hudson and his voyages of exploration in world history / Judith Edwards.
        p. cm.—(In world history)
    Includes bibliographical references and index.
    Summary: Examines the life and career of Henry Hudson, tracing his voyages in the Arctic and North America and his discovery of the Hudson River and other bodies of water during his unsuccessful search for a Northwest Passage to Asia.
    ISBN 0-7660-1885-7
    1. Hudson, Henry, d. 1611—Juvenile literature. 2. Explorers—America—Biography—Juvenile literature. 3. Explorers—Great Britain—Biography—Juvenile literature. 4. America—Discovery and exploration—English—Juvenile literature. [1. Hudson, Henry, d. 1611. 2. Explorers. 3. America—Discovery and exploration—English.] I.
Title. II. Series.

E129.H8 E38 2002
970.01'7—dc21

                                  2001004119

Printed in the United States of America

10 9 8 7 6 5 4 3 2 1

To Our Readers: We have done our best to make sure all Internet addresses in this book were active and appropriate when we went to press. However, the author and the publisher have no control over and assume no liability for the material available on those Internet sites or on other Web sites they may link to. Any comments or suggestions can be sent by e-mail to comments@enslow.com or to the address on the back cover.

Contents

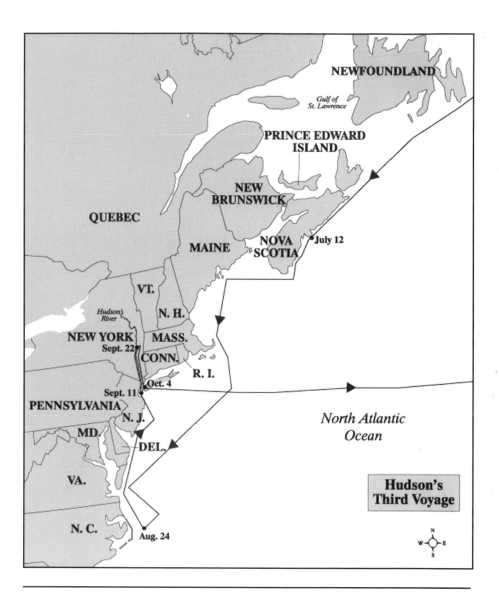

Though Henry Hudson's third voyage is known for the exploration of the Hudson River, the Half Moon *and its seamen also explored much of the northeast coast of the present-day United States.*

Chapter 1

Up a Wide, Wide River

September 3, 1609: Misty in the morning until 10 o'clock, then it cleared and the wind came to the south southeast, so we weighed anchor and sailed northward. The land is very pleasant, high and bold. At three o'clock in the afternoon we came to three great rivers.[1]

This was an ordinary entry in the logbook kept by first mate Robert Juet aboard the Dutch ship *Half Moon*. However matter-of-fact it may sound, it marked the discovery of the river known today as the Hudson.

The *Half Moon* was small for an ocean-going sailing ship, only sixty-five feet long and seventeen feet wide. It had traveled many miles from its home port in Amsterdam, Holland. The ship's captain, an English navigator named Henry Hudson, was not supposed to be anywhere near the shores of the New World. But he was determined to find a Northwest Passage to China.

This was Hudson's third voyage as a captain. The first two had been outfitted by the English Muscovy

This is a reproduction of Henry Hudson's ship the Half Moon.

Company. This trip was funded by the Dutch United East India Company. Both English and Dutch groups had hired Hudson specifically to find a North*east* Passage through the northern waters of the Arctic Ocean. Henry Hudson had secretly given up on that possibility, based on his experiences during his second voyage. So, here he was, about to sail up this wild and wide river, spurred on by a new hope—that of finding a Northwest Passage through the North American continent to Asia. This river certainly looked promising.

As Hudson and the sixteen sailors on board sailed the *Half Moon* north on this great river, they discovered that the land was not empty. It was home to many people, separated into various bands and villages. When the crew of the *Half Moon* stepped on shore, men, women, and children gathered around them. The natives gave the sailors tobacco in exchange for knives and beads. They introduced the Europeans to Indian corn baked into bread, dried currants, beans, and oysters. The sailors were intrigued by the natives' clothing of animal skins and feather cloaks, their pipes, and their jewelry made from copper.

Soon, canoes full of American Indians were paddling out to *Half Moon.* They were curious about these hairy men in odd clothing. Interested in trading, the Indians also had a tendency to pick up whatever they liked on board ship and take it away with them. Henry Hudson, writing in his journal, said that the American Indians "appear to be a friendly people, but have a great propensity to steal, and are exceedingly adroit in carrying away whatever they take a fancy to."[2]

Sailing up the mighty Hudson River, as far as what is now Albany, New York, the beauty and rich fertility of the land on either side impressed Henry Hudson and his crew with possibilities for the future. All along

The American Indians of the Hudson River would often paddle out to the Half Moon *to trade with Henry Hudson and the other members of his crew.*

the river, the *Half Moon* met canoes full of friendly Indians who wanted to come on board. These alternated with canoes full of Indians who shot deadly arrows and retreated only when the Europeans' superior gunfire drove them away. Hudson was the dinner guest of one band of natives who broke their arrows in half and threw them into the fire. They wanted to show that it was safe for Hudson to spend the night in their village.

Discovering that they ran into shallow water one hundred fifty miles up the great river, Hudson turned his ship around. As beautiful as this land was, he would not be sorry to leave the annoying American-Indian attempts to board and steal. Nor would he miss the exchange of arrows and gunfire—during which one of his crewmen and several Indians were killed. But he had not found what he was looking for—the elusive Northwest Passage. Now he was left to wonder what to do next.

Chapter 2

Who Was Henry Hudson?

Henry Hudson, sea captain and maritime explorer, made four voyages that changed European maps of the world. These voyages took place in the remarkably short space of four years. He left England on May 1, 1607, on his first voyage to find a northeastern ocean route to China. He was last seen during his final voyage, in search of a north*western* ocean route to China, on June 21, 1611.

As for documented facts about his life previous to those voyages, there are practically none. Significant dates in the lives of historical figures are usually found by consulting church registries, deeds of sale for land and farm or household equipment, personal diaries, and written recollections of people who knew the person. Unfortunately, none of those helpful documents

This portrait of Henry Hudson was painted in 1620 by Paul van Somer. Since very little is known about Hudson's life up until his first voyage, it is no surprise that artists' portraits of him differ greatly.

are available to help examine Henry Hudson's life before 1607.

The Facts About Henry Hudson

Hudson was English, and he lived in London. There are records that his wife's name was Katherine. Although Hudson's birth is not recorded, those of his three sons—Oliver, John, and Richard—are. He was a friend of Captain John Smith, another ardent explorer and one of the founders of the Jamestown settlement in the area called Virginia on the North American coast.

Beyond these, there are some facts that are *probable* about Hudson's life. These are called conjectures, because they fit with the few known facts, but have not been proven. Henry Hudson was probably the son of a prominent citizen and alderman, a member of the local London government, Henry Hudson the elder. The younger Hudson may have had relatives among the merchants who formed the Muscovy Company, his English employers for the first two voyages to find a Northeast Passage. He undoubtedly had years of seagoing experience before 1607. We know this because of the exceptional navigational skills the journals of his voyages show. He may have even been a crew member on a 1587 voyage that sailed near an intriguing ocean phenomenon of whirling waters in the Atlantic Ocean to the north of North America.[1] This was called the Furious Overfall by Captain John Davis, another maritime explorer who was searching for the Northwest Passage. Hudson was eager to explore it on his own voyages. But this is where conjecture, often based on what would make sense if it were true, sets in. There is no written proof that Hudson made *any* voyages before 1607.

We do not even know what Henry Hudson really looked like. Although portraits were later painted of him, historians know of no picture or drawing that was made during his lifetime. Nor was any physical description of him written down. With the exception of the few indisputable facts, what we know about Hudson comes from the ship's logs and the official correspondence surrounding his four voyages.

An Image Emerges

Still, a "picture" of Hudson does emerge. We can form an image of the explorer through the course of events, the comments of others, and the record of his actions. We learn about Henry Hudson's personality, his relations with crew members, his leadership style, and his stubbornness, persistence, and courage. Together, these bits of evidence show us a real, and extremely complex, person.

This picture, however, brings up more questions than answers. Why was Henry Hudson, so skilled a navigator and so determined to find a Northwest Passage to Asia, always in trouble with his crew? Did his single-minded goal make him lose touch with the human needs of his sailors? And why, when confronted with mutinous situations—when crew members threatened to take over the ship—where a show of strength was needed, did he back down? These questions come to mind as one reads through the pages of Hudson's ship logs and journals, though very few pages of Hudson's own journal still exist. All these questions about Hudson and his voyages remain fascinating, unsolved mysteries.

Chapter 3

The World of Henry Hudson

Most of the information known today about the voyages of Henry Hudson comes from a book called *Purchas, His Pilgrimes.*[1] Reverend Samuel Purchas put together journals and records, previously published in *The Principal Navigations* (1589) by English historian Richard Hakluyt. In this book appeared letters, contracts, and other documents about important navigators. *Purchas, His Pilgrimes* was not printed until 1625, and even before *The Principal Navigations,* Hudson's own journals of the voyages were not available. Both Hudson's 1609 voyage to North America and his 1610 voyage to the very far north of that continent involved mutinies. Therefore, historians speculate that the mutineers destroyed any journal pages that might prove their guilt.[2]

Just after Hudson's last voyage, many Dutch writers published material about his journeys. Richard Hakluyt's ambitious book drew together the logs and journals of all "great traffiques and discoveries" for a fifteen hundred–year period.[3] Hakluyt's earlier book, *Diverse Voyages,* printed in 1582, called attention to the possibility of finding a Northwest Passage through North America to Asia. Hudson was influenced in his search for a Northwest Passage by this *Diverse Voyages,* as well as by later maps and Hakluyt's writings. These included navigator John Davis's detailed accounts of his voyages.

The Northwest Passage

Anyone who has studied American history has heard of the Northwest Passage, a water route rumored to cross the North American continent from the Atlantic Ocean to the Pacific Ocean. The search for this passage, however, was preceded by a search for a Northeast Passage—a water route going through or around Russia eastward toward the Pacific Ocean. Both of these hoped-for water routes were supposed to lead to "Cathay"—a medieval term for China, as well as other territories of the Far East, or Asia.

As far back as the travels of the Venetian explorer Marco Polo, described in *The Book of Ser Marco Polo* written in 1298, the Far East had been the source of tantalizing exotic and new additions to European culture. Tales were told of silks, spices, jewels, riches, and luxuries beyond measure. An overland trade route from China, India, and the Far East flourished before the mid-fifteenth century.

When the Turks conquered Constantinople in 1453, however, the overland route was closed to all but the most foolhardy European adventurers. Finding a water route to the Far East became most important in the minds of European kings. But before Christopher Columbus voyaged to the West, very little was really understood about how the earth looked.

What the Greeks and Romans Thought

The ancient Greek philosopher Plato believed that there were many underground seas that fed rivers and lakes. These bodies of water supposedly emptied into the above-ground oceans. This was called the concept of indrawing seas. Plato and other ancient Greeks believed that all the world's waters were connected to each other and flowed continually. Land masses were believed to be balanced from one side of the world to the other, surrounded by these indrawing seas, which emptied into the polar oceans.

Sixteenth-century cartographers drew maps depicting these islands, describing the seas that separated them as "dividing all the countries as they flow into the circle of the world from the outer oceans."[4] Thus, if there was a balance between land and water, there had to be a Northeast or a Northwest Passage from Europe to the riches of the Far East. This belief inspired countless sea and land explorations for three centuries after Columbus made his trips to America.

The search for these passages, however, was filled with dangers—both real and imagined. Horrible rocks and ice could crush ships with no warning. Legends told of monsters such as giant squids that could

With his 1492 voyage to the West Indies (just south of Florida), Christopher Columbus changed the way Henry Hudson and other future explorers would view the world.

squeeze ships in their tentacles, or the kraken, which had spiky horns that could pierce a ship. There were stories of seas of mud left by the legendary continent of Atlantis, which was supposed to have sunk beneath the ocean in ancient times. Sailing too far south, it was believed, would make a sailor's blood boil, and going too far north would cause it to freeze. With dangers such as these believed as facts, it is a wonder that any voyages were undertaken.

The Lure of Cathay

Promises of riches beyond all imagination lured voyagers onto the dangerous oceans. Although the overland travel route was closed to Europe when the Turks conquered Constantinople, the sea was not controlled by a fierce people. New water routes would allow Europeans to have access once again to the riches of the Far East.

Although voyages of the Celts and Vikings (peoples from the northern British Isles and from Scandinavia) provided some information about the Atlantic Ocean, this was combined with the concept of indrawing seas and balanced land masses. If a ship were to sail across the Atlantic, people believed, it would surely reach the large continent containing Cathay—or Asia. No one had the foggiest idea that a whole new world existed, an unexpected land mass between Europe and Asia, until Columbus discovered it. However, when Columbus landed at the West

Indies south of North America, he thought he had found the islands of Japan.[5]

Even before Columbus came near to the southern shores of North America, Spain and Portugal controlled passage on the Atlantic in the Southern Hemisphere. But when Columbus stumbled on this unexpected and large land mass, while flying under the Spanish flag, Spain expanded its empire to the Caribbean Sea. The Aztec Empire in Mexico was conquered by Hernándo Cortés in 1519. Ferdinand Magellan, also in 1519, sailed west from Spain to find a passage to the Moluccas, islands where trading for spices was profitable. The Spanish established a presence in the Caribbean, Florida, Mexico, and South America. Meanwhile, the Portuguese explored and established trading colonies as far south as the Atlantic coast of Africa. Their navigators sailed around the Cape of Good Hope and reached India, China, and Japan. Because of the need for favorable winds to get them where they wanted to go, mariners were often driven far off course. This led to the discovery of Madeira, the Cape Verde Islands, and the Azores.

At this time, great power was held by the Catholic Church in Rome. Since it was a worldwide power, the Pope could decide who "owned" various parts of these newly discovered lands. Spain and Portugal were both Catholic countries, and each petitioned Rome on the grounds that it would be taking the work of the church to the new world. Pope Nicholas V issued a document in 1455 that gave Portugal the right to conquer and take over all the land along the Atlantic coast of Africa. A second document, issued by Pope Calixtus III, gave Portugal the lands of Guinea, the Madeiras, the Azores, and the Cape Verdes. Since Spain at that time was issued only the Canary Islands, various petitions and treaties passed between Rome and the rulers of the two countries. Finally, in 1494, the line was drawn. In the Treaty of Tordesillas, it was agreed that:

> . . . a boundary or straight line be determined and drawn north and south, from pole to pole, on the Ocean Sea, from the Arctic to the Antarctic Pole. This line shall be drawn straight . . . at a distance of 370 leagues west of the Cape Verde Islands. And all lands on the eastern side of the said bound . . . shall belong to the said King of Portugal and his successors. And all other lands shall belong to the said King and Queen of Castile.[6]

Explorers such as Vasco da Gama and Magellan pushed these boundaries until this division of the globe into east and west again ran into trouble. Significant conquests by Spain in Mexico and South America, and Portugal's solid trade routes around the Cape of Good Hope, effectively controlled the oceans south of the Canary Islands. What would the rest of Western Europe—countries with rulers and subjects who wanted a piece of the wealth generated by Spanish and Portuguese trade empires—do?

Once again, the story returns to the search for a northern passage to Asia. Spain and Portugal did not control the northern latitudes. During the reign of

King Henry VII of England, a father and son named John and Sebastian Cabot came to prominence. John Cabot, who was born in Genoa and grew up in Venice (both principalities that would later be part of Italy), had emigrated to England as a young man. By 1497, he was a successful merchant who convinced other wealthy merchants to supply him with men and ships to explore the seas of the north. He would find new lands—and the celebrated, elusive Northern Passage. In fact, it was John Cabot who originated the idea of a Northwest, instead of a Northeast Passage.[7]

Though Cabot did not find the Northwest Passage, he discovered Newfoundland, named so because it was a "new-found land" (though it is believed that Portuguese fishermen had already discovered it and been fishing there), and claimed it for the English king. On a second voyage, with five ships at Cabot's disposal, only one ship returned to England, shortly after departure. The other four were lost, including the one on which John Cabot had sailed.

The result of Cabot's first voyage was to open up the fishing banks off Newfoundland, where fish were the only creatures in control of the seas. Soon, word of this extensive opportunity for fishing sent English ships to the "new world." It "sparked England's claim to the entire North American continent."[8]

It was John Cabot's son, Sebastian, who would draw on his charts "an unbroken coast-line between Labrador and Florida."[9] During the second Cabot voyage, in which John Cabot lost his life, Sebastian

Cabot became aware of two northern straits, now called the Hudson and Davis straits. He believed that the Northwest Passage lay somewhere through those two difficult waterways. Sebastian Cabot's 1508 voyage failed to find this passage. However, his explorations along the entire coast of North America solidified beyond any doubt the existence of this large, unbroken land mass that lay dauntingly between Europe and Asia.

Spanish and Portuguese navigators had already discovered that no passage to Asia existed through South America. Now, the rest of Europe realized the passage was not to be found near Newfoundland. Could there be a river or strait that ran through the middle of this new continent?

A New World

It was not until 1524 that another navigator was able to convince a group of merchants that he could find this Northwest Passage. Giovanni da Verrazano, a Florentine navigator sailing for France under the auspices of a group of French and Florentine merchants, believed that the middle of the continent held hope for a passage to Asia.

Verrazano explored the North American coastline from the Carolinas, coming close to but not discovering Chesapeake and Delaware bays, and entering New York Harbor. He saw but did not explore the river up which Hudson would travel. He named New York's Upper Bay after the French king's sister, calling it

Santa Margarita. His ship then turned north toward Newfoundland. He returned to Europe, corroborating Sebastian Cabot's claim that this was one big piece of land.

No longer could Europeans believe that there were two continents with lots of water surrounding them. It seemed like there was more land than water in the world, and that this new continent was perhaps the largest of all. From the southern end of South America to the northern tip of North America, near the North Pole, lay a coastline that appeared to be impenetrable by any ship seeking to sail to the Pacific from the Atlantic.

The Catholic Church, which in the middle of the sixteenth century had strong ties to the French King Francis I, changed its decree on who owned what lands. Pope Clement VII stated that if a new land was discovered by another sovereign nation, it was fair game to claim it. Subsequently, Jacques Cartier led three expeditions to North America, concentrating on finding a Northwest Passage through the Gulf of St. Lawrence at the far north of North America. He, as others before him, was unsuccessful. He explored farther inland than earlier voyagers, and his findings led other navigators, including Hudson, to believe that a passage might lie farther to the north, in the arctic regions.

Sebastian Cabot, who had published his charts of the North American coastline, enjoyed prominence for his findings. As early as 1515, Cabot's findings were agreed to by a Spanish cartographer named Petrus Martyr, who believed there must be a passage *through* the new continent. Unable to get the English king to fund another ocean search, Cabot went to Spain. There, he found employment as a cartographer and the director of a maritime school. He even led a voyage to the Moluccas in 1526. This expedition, however, was not successful.

The Frozen North

Sebastian Cabot, who was, according to historian Llewelyn Powys, a smart man who had learned to survive in the politics of his day, finally returned to England in 1548. He now had another idea. Along with Peter Plancius, a Dutch geographer who believed that if one sailed far enough north the waters would actually be warm, and Robert Thorne, a merchant who promoted voyages to the north, Cabot advocated sailing directly across the North Pole.[10] Surely there would be open waters in this region. He was able to convince a group of one hundred London merchants to mount an expedition to find a North*east* Passage to Cathay.

Cabot was the major planner of this expedition. Sir Hugh Willoughby headed a fleet of three ships that sailed north to the Kara Sea. Despite careful planning and Cabot's navigational expertise (though he did not sail with the ships), the trip was two parts disaster and one part good business. Two of the ships were frozen into the ice above Novaya Zemlya. A search party, sent after the two ships a year later, found all the crew members, including Sir Hugh Willoughby, frozen "in various postures, like statues, as if they had been adjusted and placed in those attitudes."[11] This information was written in a letter by Giovanni Michiel, the Venetian ambassador, who had heard of the crew's terrible fate from Stephen Burroughs, captain of the rescue vessel.

Burroughs, captain of the third ship, had sailed to the Russian coast on the White Sea. Wintering in the town of Archangel, the ship's pilot Richard Chancellor led a small group of men on foot to Moscow, where he negotiated with Ivan Vasilyevich, better known as Ivan the Terrible, to set up trade relations with England. To the English, who very much wanted to sell woolen goods to northern people whose winters required warmth, this was a most desirable outcome. Burroughs would once again, in 1556, be sent by the Muscovy Company to find a northern route to Cathay. Ice in the Kara Sea, as before, stopped his progress, and the Muscovy Company settled down to trade with Russia until the early seventeenth century.

Other groups of merchants in London financed several expeditions to find the Northwest Passage in the late years of the sixteenth century. Martin Frobisher led three voyages—1576, 1577, 1578—that expanded what was known about the arctic regions of North America. John Davis sailed three times starting in 1585, encountering what he called the Furious Overfall that roared "lothsomely crying like the rage

Source Document

The second of July they fell with the coast of Florida in shoal water, where they felt a most delicate sweet smell, though they saw no land, which ere long they espied, thinking it the continent: an hundred feet and twenty miles they sailed not finding any harbour. The first that appeared with much difficulty they entered, and anchored; and after thanks to God they went to view the next land adjoining, to take possession of it for the Queen's most excellent Majesty. . . .[12]

Captain John Smith described the discovery of Virginia in 1576.

of the waters under the London bridge."[13] This was at the entrance to what would be called Hudson Bay. Early in Davis's trip he had sailed along the coast of Greenland, known from Norse sagas, which are folktales from Scandinavian countries. He also explored a bay of Baffin Island north of North America, previously found by Frobisher but not recognized by Davis, and renamed it Lumley's Inlet. Davis surmised that, though he had not found the Northwest Passage, the bay that would be called Hudson Bay or Lumley's Inlet most probably held this elusive prize.

Though there was no telegraph, telephone, or television in the late sixteenth century, word did spread that the possibility of a Northeast or Northwest Passage still remained. It was not only the English merchants who wanted to be first to find it. William Barents, sailing under the Dutch flag, believed that the passage could be found by sailing north of a large island called Novaya Zemlya, near the North Pole. Peter Plancius urged Barents, about to undertake his third trip to the arctic regions, to travel farther north before heading east. Barents discovered a northern land he called Bear Island, because of the polar bears he encountered there—the first ever seen. But he also encountered the usual and terrible block for sailors to

Henry Hudson and other Europeans did not even know polar bears existed until they started exploring the Arctic.

the northern regions—ice. He was forced to spend the winter on Novaya Zemlya and died there. He had contributed valuable information about the polar regions, and a cartographer named Baptista van Doetechum created a map of Barents's final exploratory voyage.

The logbooks of information and disinformation from all of these intrepid, and often tragically lost, navigators were available to the next adventurer to northern waters. Combined with writings by Martyr, Plancius, and Hakluyt, and maps by Jodocus Hondius, Gerardus Mercator, and Abraham Ortelius, some guidelines for future voyages existed. In 1607, the Muscovy Company outfitted a ship called the *Hopewell.* Its captain's assignment was to find a Northeast Passage to Asia by sailing north, right across the North Pole. That captain was Henry Hudson.

Chapter 4

Is It Really Warm at the North Pole?

On April 19, 1607, a group of eleven men and a boy attended religious services in London, at the church of St. Ethelburga. This church, which replaced an even more ancient church on the same spot near Bishopsgate, in London, was built in the fifteenth century. In 1607, the church was in a busy section of the city, with shops, hotels, and taverns. Names of streets around the area included Wormwood Alley and Peahen Alley, with taverns named the Four Swans, the Queens Head, the Green Dragon, and the Black Bull. This was a typical section of the old city of London, and often the scene of religious ceremonies held for men who were about to tackle unknown and dangerous seas. On this date, it was the scene of the departure ceremonies for Captain Henry Hudson, his son, and his crew.

Reasons for the Voyage

After fifty years, the Muscovy Company decided to send an expedition to find the Northeast Passage. Trade with Russia, for many years exclusive to the English, had been interrupted in the early years of the seventeenth century by energetic Dutch involvement. Russia, too, was becoming interested in entering the race for new global discoveries.

According to conjecture, Henry Hudson must have pushed for renewing the search for a shorter, northern sea route to Asia. Eighty years earlier, Robert Thorne, a merchant and a geographer, had petitioned King Henry VIII to outfit an expedition across the North Pole, saying that "There is no land uninhabitable and no sea unnavigable."[1] The idea was that since the sun shone for five months at the North Pole, the ground would be sufficiently warmed to keep the ice calm during the dark months. Peter Plancius agreed with this saying, "If a small fire is kept lighted in a room all the time, the warmth of the room will be more easily maintained than by means of a large fire that is constantly allowed to go out."[2]

Thorne was destined not to convince the Muscovy Company at that time, when Russian trade was making merchants rich. It was under different economic circumstances that Henry Hudson proposed his trip. Captain John Smith, a possible choice for heading a voyage of discovery, had already been hired by a group of wealthy backers who formed the London Company.

John Smith was a candidate for heading the voyage that Henry Hudson would eventually lead. Smith instead was hired by the London Company to start a new colony in North America. He founded a settlement at Jamestown, Virginia, in 1607.

He would join a group of merchant adventurers to found a new colony in North America, at Jamestown.

Hudson Departs

A crew composed of Hudson, his young son John, first mate John Colman, and nine seamen set out from Gravesend, England, on May 1, 1607. They were heading north—far, far north.

The Shetland Islands, a group of islands north of Scotland, were the first sounding of land, on May 26. "Soundings" of the bottom of the sea were taken using a scoop device, which brought up a "blacke, ozie, sandie" bottom containing a few yellow shells.[3]

By June 13, the *Hopewell* was near Greenland. Previously, on June 11, the men had seen whales playing near their ship. As they traveled north of Greenland, the land was bleak. A journal kept by John Pleyce (also spelled Playse in some literature) recorded this bleakness: "Our sayle and shrouds did freeze. . . . all the afternoone and all the evening it rained. . . ."[4]

Snow swirled around the ship making visibility so poor that the ship had to "lay to," that is, point into the wind and more or less float still in the water.

Hudson noticed that the current was "setting toward the southwest."[5] The men were experiencing a current that brings driftwood from Siberia to the Inuit (Eskimos), which is needed for fires.[6]

Three whales showed up near the *Hopewell* on June 18. None of them bothered the small ship. Hudson continued to sail northeast, trying to find a sea that had no ice clogging it. The ship was again near the coast of Greenland, but Henry Hudson was not sure of this. He believed he had found yet another land mass. He called it "Hold-with-Hope."[7] He felt that the climate was getting better, in keeping with the theory that the seas were warm at the North Pole.

We have no way of knowing what Hudson felt when he encountered yet more land, when he had hoped to find open sea. He continued to take note of his surroundings. In his journal, he noted that on the land he called Hold-with-Hope, the crew saw unusual birds with white stomachs and black backs, but built like ducks. These were probably great auks, a bird that is now extinct.[8]

The weather continued to be stormy. Ice impeded the ship's forward motion. Strange mammals such as the grampus, a member of the dolphin family, surrounded the ship. By July 6, the crew steered into a "very green sea," which gave them hope.[9] But on setting sail once again, land and ice surrounded them. Seals swam around the ship, sunning themselves on the islands of ice.

The land the men had spotted on June 27 is now named Spitzbergen. Hudson referred to it as Newland. By the time they had negotiated the ice floes and come into the "green sea," they were uncertain of their position.[10] The men used driftwood to make repairs to the *Hopewell.*

All around the *Hopewell,* in a bay that would be called Whale Bay, were immense whales, which looked like giant fish. On July 14, one huge whale dove under the ship's keel, but then swam away without doing any damage.

Journey to the Far North

The same day the whale played with the *Hopewell,* four of Hudson's crewmen went ashore on this "high and ragged land" and found much animal and bird life.[11] They found freshwater streams and were sorry they did not have a good way to bring back water for the crew.[12] Though the weather was calm when the men went on shore, it quickly became stormy. The *Hopewell* sailed back and forth waiting for the flimsy ship's boat to bring the four crewmen back, which it finally did.

The weather gave them no choice but to sail northeast. This brought the *Hopewell* to a part of the coast of Greenland called the Seven Icebergs. Here, glaciers—large bodies of ice that either move slowly down a slope or valley or spread on a land surface—rise with a greenish blue color, beautiful and daunting.

We now get a picture of this very small ship floundering in the floating ice far north of England. Hudson, according to the trust accorded him by the Muscovy Company, was an expert navigator. But he, too, was floundering. Where would they go next?

The *Hopewell* and its captain and crew were definitely far to the north. The next land they sighted is now called Amsterdam Island. Hudson named its farthest northern cape Hakluyt's Headland, after

Henry Hudson and his expedition were in awe of the immense glaciers of Greenland. Often, ships had to be careful of the large chunks of ice that would break off as a glacier slowly flowed into the sea.

Richard Hakluyt, who had dedicated his life to preserving records of navigators' searches for a passage to Asia.

The logbook entry at this time, written by seaman John Pleyce, is hard to read—because the crewmen really did not know where they were. Hudson had wanted to get so far north that he could actually sail across the warm waters of the North Pole. He hoped to sail "straight across the Pole to China," explained historian Llewelyn Powys.[13] When he went as far north as the *Hopewell* could get, however, he was confronted with nothing but ice. Perhaps he could go around Spitzbergen to the south and try to go north again on its eastern coast.

The disappointed crew sailed south for four days, noting the many seals, whose furs could bring a profit for English ships. Turning westward, the ship was once again tossed by severe storms, and on July 27, the crew realized that "the sea was pushing us westward toward the ice."[14] The ship's boat was lowered and the men rowed hard, towing the *Hopewell* through the high seas. Luck gave the ship a wind that sent the boat southeast, away from the ice that would have crushed the ship and its crew. Once again, the men wished they had a larger ship's boat with long oars that could be used to tow the boat out of trouble.[15]

Failure to Find the Passage

Hudson discovered, by observing the icy coastline, that there was no passage to the Northeast to be found where he was looking. Extreme cold alternated with foggy conditions, and on July 29, he and his crew arrived at the southern tip of Spitzbergen. Sailing south down the coast, the sailors marveled that the land was somewhat habitable and not covered with snow. But the season was advancing, and it was time to set sail for England. They would have to leave the discovery of that elusive Northeast Passage for another trip. The *Hopewell* arrived at the Faeroe Islands, which lie northwest of the British Isles, on August 15.

It took the homeward-bound *Hopewell* another month to arrive at the dock on the Thames River in England.

By the time Hudson returned to England, his logbooks and place names show that he had traveled very far west of the course he had originally planned to take. "The most likely explanation is that he intended to make an attempt to find the Northwest Passage" in this 1607 voyage, according to writer and cartographer Donald Johnson.[16]

Though Hudson did not find the Northeast or Northwest Passage, and did not bring back valuable cargo or even a hold full of fish, his voyage was very important to English navigation. He had proven that the waters at the North Pole were not warm as had been believed. In fact, the tremendous quantity of ice jutting out from the land and floating in the sea made it totally impossible to sail across the Pole. The Muscovy Company, however, would profit from Hudson's discoveries in another way.

Chapter 5

Whales and Walrus Beware!

The report of numerous whales off the coast of Spitzbergen led to a large, highly profitable industry in by-products of whales, particularly for lamp oil that was made from their blubber (fat). These large mammals, so unafraid of humans that they lolled alongside the *Hopewell,* were killed in the hundreds of thousands over the next few centuries.

An island Hudson had discovered on his westward course back to England, which he named Hudson's Tutches, brought about walrus hunting. Thousands upon thousands of these playful, awkward animals were killed for their tusks, which were used to make tools and beautiful objects. Their hides were used to make leather, and their blubber to make oil for lamps. Once the whales and walrus were almost wiped out in the waters of these cold, uninhabitable lands, the

Henry Hudson and his crew often saw whales during their four voyages on the open seas.

islands once again became barren, filled only with ice and snow.

Another Try to Find the Passage

The Muscovy Company evidently believed that Henry Hudson deserved another try at finding the Northeast Passage. This time, however, he would take a different route. It had been proven that sailing directly across the North Pole was not possible. No warm seas greeted explorers there. But several other theories were still untested.

One of the problems facing navigators in these far northern waters was that the maps and charts from which they worked were flawed. Since no one had actually *been* as far north as they believed the Northeast Passage to be, cartographers (map makers) had to rely on the logbooks and charts of navigators who had been thrashing around in fog and stormy seas. A part of a coastline would loom, their reckoning by compass would be thrown off, and the captain would declare he had found a new land. For instance, the large land mass of Greenland kept getting "discovered" and called by new names, as did Spitzbergen and Novaya Zemlya, not to mention smaller islands. This was confusing, to say the least.

Hudson sailed with the 1594 map by Peter Plancius, based on a 1569 map by Gerardus Mercator. Both maps had mistakes, showing possible passages through arctic waters wider than they actually were. Every time a new hunk of land was discovered, variations had to be made in previous maps to make room for the new discoveries. Greenland, in particular, jumped around quite a bit. Once thought to be part of Asia, it gradually became an island, though still not in the right place, by the end of the sixteenth century.

When Hudson decided to travel north to Novaya Zemlya and try to find a passage north of the island or through it to the Kara Sea, he was navigating by maps that had many wrong latitude and longitude markings. He was also going into the bitterly cold and icy territory that had killed Sir Hugh Willoughby and

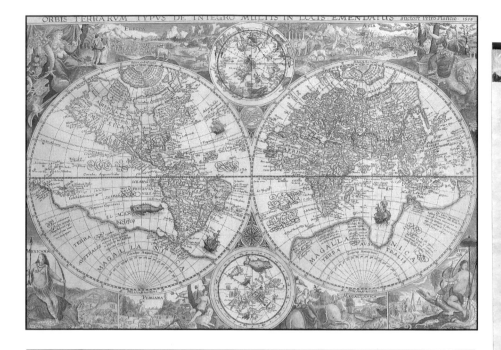

Henry Hudson sailed with a 1594 map by Peter Plancius. Here is a map Plancius created in 1599.

numerous others. Hudson thought that if he could find a passage north of Novaya Zemlya, he would sail east along the Siberian coastline, at the far east of Russia, until he arrived at the Pacific Ocean. Failing that, he would explore the old legend of a passage through the River Ob at the west of Russia. This river, with its mystical-sounding name, empties into the Kara Sea from the northern shore of Russia, east of Novaya Zemlya. It had long been rumored that the sea beyond Ob was warm, making a passage to the Pacific easy.

Hudson Sets Sail

Setting out from London on April 22, 1608, Hudson sailed on the same ship, the *Hopewell*. This time, however, he had an improved ship's boat. The crew had four more men than the first voyage. However, only two sailors from the 1607 voyage and Hudson's son John returned for the second trip. The first mate was a man named Robert Juet, who would sail with Hudson on his remaining voyages. Juet was, by all accounts, an odd choice for second in command. He was "an elderly man, cynical, skeptical and dangerous," according to historian Llewelyn Powys.[1]

The *Hopewell* sailed north from London through the North Sea. In a month, it passed near the west coast of Norway. Several of the crew had fallen sick, and the ship was mired in fog and cold. It was hardly a good beginning for this new and hopeful trip.

On this trip, Henry Hudson himself was the sole writer of the ship's journal. On May 25, he described their situation: "Today the weather was clear, but searching cold; the cold began on the twenty-first, at which time my carpenter became sick, and still is."[2]

Luckily, the carpenter, Philip Staffe, recovered by June 4 and made a mast for the new ship's boat. The rest of the crew made the sail. By June 7, the *Hopewell*, sailing north, had encountered snow and ice, the first of the journey, which led Hudson to turn the ship south. The men faced rough weather until June 15.

A Mermaid Sighting?

On that day, two members of the crew supposedly spotted a mermaid. Hudson wrote about this at length in his journal. He described how the men saw this phenomenon: "Her back and breasts were like a woman's, her body as big as ours, her skin very white, and she had long, black hair hanging down behind."[3] Of course, she had the usual fish tail—described to be like that of a porpoise, and speckled.

Did Hudson and the other sailors really believe in mermaids? The answer is yes. Sightings of mermaids had been recorded as early as the sixth century. In the

Source Document

Now also I will not omit to relate something of a strange Creature that I first saw there in the yeere 1610, in a morning early as I was standing by the water side, in the Harbour of Saint Johns, which I espied verie swiftly to come swimming towards me, looking cheerefully, as it had beene a woman, by the Face, Eyes, Nose, Mouth, Chin, eares, Necke, and Forehead: It seemed to be so beautifull. . . . This (I suppose) was a Mermaide.[4]

Sailors of Henry Hudson's day believed in many fanciful creatures, including mermaids.

fifteenth century, a mermaid was reported to have been washed through a hole in a dyke in Holland. This one supposedly lived with humans long enough to learn to spin and to become Christian![5] In that same century, a merman was spotted, and yet another mermaid. It would be interesting to know what sort of creature the spotters had really seen.

The Journey Continues

The *Hopewell* was once again proceeding north, but ice drove the ship back. A tremendous roaring was heard, which the crew believed to be made by polar bears. Forced to turn southeastward, Hudson was now approaching the long island of Nova Zembla, called Novaya Zemlya by Russians, and still known by that name today.

Many seamen often claimed they saw mermaids swimming through the choppy waves of the Atlantic Ocean.

It had become apparent that the way north between Spitzbergen and Novaya Zemlya was blocked by ice. There was no passage to be found by sailing north. Hudson would have to find a passage through the island.

Sailing south, the *Hopewell* anchored about two miles from the shore of Novaya Zemlya, in reasonably good seas. Hudson sent Robert Juet, boatswain John Cooke, and four other crewmen ashore to explore and bring back fresh water.

The men saw grass, felt the sun, and found many streams of melting snow. Bears, deer, and foxes left footprints on the snow. The men brought back to the ship whales' fins and the dung and horns of deer. When the exploratory party returned to the ship, the entire crew saw walrus swimming around them.

Hunting for a Profit

Hudson, mindful of the Muscovy Company's desire to make a profit, wanted to bring something valuable home—just in case he did not find the Northeast Passage. He sent Juet and several others on shore to find the walrus. There was no sign of these large creatures on shore, but the men again saw many animal footprints. They also found a large wooden cross, left there by some unknown traveler. When the boat returned to the ship, it was loaded with birds and eggs—but no walrus heads.

Finally, walrus were sighted on shore, and everyone but Hudson and his son went on shore to kill them. One unlucky walrus was killed and his head brought back to the ship.

The men then explored more of the island and brought back more birds. At midnight, the ship's anchor broke free and the ship "went aground." That is, it ran into water not deep enough for it to float. With difficulty, the crew pulled the ship back to sea, probably using the ship's boat, only to find more ice.

The Search Goes on

Hudson, unable to pass between Spitzbergen and Novaya Zemlya, had thought he might pass south of Novaya Zemlya, north of the River Ob. Since the ice was flowing toward them, however, that was impossible.

By July 4, the ship was in a large space of water with a strong current. The ship's boat set out, once again with Juet and five men, to navigate a stream that flowed north. Could this be the River Ob?

The boat came back the next day, having navigated a river that became more and more shallow the farther north the men went. Although Hudson reported that Novaya Zemlya, seen at its best season of the year, was pleasant and without a great deal of snow, he realized that ice was again the enemy. Many rivers and streams on the island create ice in the colder parts of the year. Hudson wrote matter-of-factly, "By means of all that ice, I suppose there will be no navigable passage this way."[6]

For the rest of the trip, Hudson pursued a westerly direction, though he may still have been looking for

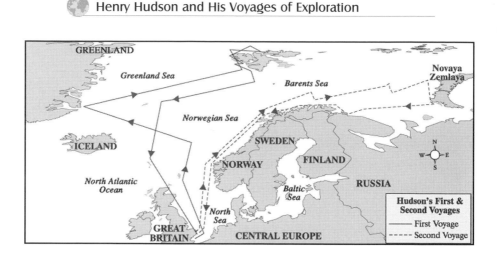

Henry Hudson and his crew sailed through the Greenland, Norwegian, and Barents Seas during his first and second voyages to find a Northeast Passage.

any possible way to sail east to Asia. On August 7, an entry in his journal mentioned that something happened to make Hudson change his course for home: "I used all diligence to arrive at London, and therefore I now gave my crew a certificate under my hand, of my free and willing return, without persuasion or force by any one or more of them."[7] Had a mutiny—or the threat of one—occurred? From the language of Hudson's writings, it seems certain.

Hudson went on to say that, since he had not been able to find the Northeast Passage by the means he had hoped, he "therefore resolved to use all means I could to sail to the northwest."[8] He would now try heading toward the Furious Overfall, called so by Captain John Davis. Since he was not able to get as near that goal due to "contrary winds," he bowed to common sense—and most probably to his crew's insistence—and returned to Gravesend, on the River Thames, about twenty-two miles from London, on August 26. Now he would have to hope the Muscovy Company would agree to let him try once more.

The Dutch East India Company to the Rescue

Politics has always played a large part in the relations between people—especially where matters of money and power are concerned. Politics, besides being the art or science of government, refers to the competition between interest groups or individuals for power.

Europe in the sixteenth and seventeenth centuries was a storm of politics. Maneuvering to find and control the sea routes to the riches of Asia had resulted in Spain and Portugal's dominance over the Southern Hemisphere. The other European countries were not willing to remain in the background without a share in the prosperity. Those governments began competing to identify new sea routes, discover new lands, and especially, to find a Northeast or a Northwest Passage to Asia.

The Dutch Enter the Competition for the Seas

In the sixteenth century, the Netherlands was a loosely formed group of provinces with a common language but no centralized government. The Spanish dominated the Dutch political system and religion. Many people lost their lives in battles for independence from Spanish rule. Finally, in 1579, southern Belgian provinces in what would eventually become Holland, joined together to form the Republic of the Seven United Provinces. This region declared its freedom from Spanish dominance. However, it took until 1609, barely five days before Henry Hudson's third voyage began, for Spain to sign a formal treaty recognizing that independence.

Dutch ships then raided Spanish ships returning from the New World with silver and gold and other imports. The new Holland also built a large shipping empire that sailed to the Baltics and traded and fished around the coasts of England, Scotland, Greenland, Spain, and France. Because of a trade agreement with Portugal, Dutch ships sailed into Lisbon and filled their holds with the spices craved by other European countries. In 1580, the Portuguese government was taken over by Spain, and Dutch access to Lisbon was stopped. An expedition to directly reach Java—southernmost of the Indonesian Islands south of China—by sailing around the Cape of Good Hope left Holland in 1595. Captain Cornelius de Houtman was successful in reaching the Indies—islands in the Indian Ocean—and other Dutch ships soon followed.

Because of the continuing difficulties of competing with ships from other countries and the ever-active pirates from the islands of Malaysia, Dutch merchants banded together in 1602 to form one large company called the *De Verenigde Oost-Indische Compagnie,* or VOC. It is known in the English language as the Dutch East India Company. This powerful organization of already powerful commercial ventures boasted forty large ships, a great number of smaller ships, five thousand sailors, and six hundred cannons. The VOC was wealthier than the Muscovy Company, which had sponsored Henry Hudson on his first two voyages. The government of Holland, called the States-General, granted the VOC a twenty-one-year charter giving the company complete rights to the route east around the Cape of Good Hope and west through the Strait of Magellan in South America. The charter did not prohibit sailing through a northern passage, nor did it make any provision that discovery of that new route would be exclusive to the company.

Hudson Turns to the Dutch

The Dutch desire to find that new route and declare it for Holland, brings us back to Henry Hudson, the English navigator. The Muscovy Company was not interested in sending Hudson on yet another trip to the clearly frozen Arctic region in search of a Northeast Passage. Despite the commercial success brought to England by the discovery of large breeding grounds of whales and walrus, Hudson had been unsuccessful in raising money for a third voyage. But word that he had sailed farther north than any other navigator, within 10 degrees of the North Pole, was circulating around Europe.

Emmanuel van Meteren, the Dutch consul (representative of his government) in London, arranged for Hudson to travel to Amsterdam, in the Netherlands. Before leaving London, Hudson attended a ceremony for the christening of a granddaughter, Alice, the child of his oldest son, Oliver, on September 18, 1608. This is one of the very few personal biographical facts we know about Hudson, and it tells us that he did not leave for Holland, where he arrived near the end of 1608, until after September 18.[1]

When Hudson arrived in Amsterdam and met with the directors of the Dutch East India Company, they were cool toward his proposal to attempt once again to sail across the North Pole. Some people still believed that if a navigator steered toward the open sea, the very depth of the water would prevent ice formation, and the water would get warmer if he got near enough to the Pole. The directors of the company did not laugh at this idea. However, the failure of William Barents's third expedition, under the Dutch flag, to discover this Northeast Passage north of Novaya Zemlya—and his subsequent death on that inhospitable hunk of land—certainly put them off. The directors told Hudson to return the next year, when they would consider sending him north.

Friends in High Places

For Hudson, this delay was not acceptable. This complex man, who was no rough and uneducated seaman, had powerful friends among the leading cartographers and geographers of the era. Peter Plancius, a theologian, intellectual, and as obsessed with finding a northern passage to Asia as Hudson was, lived in Amsterdam. Plancius had started a school of navigation, and William Barents had been one of his pupils. Plancius was the official cartographer of the Dutch East India Company. He produced nearly eighty maps for them. Hudson confided to Plancius his true intentions about where his voyage would take him.[2] This is known because his words and a map that Hudson drew for Plancius showing the route he wanted to take was shared with another mapmaker, Hessel Gerritz, several years later.[3]

Another friend who helped champion Hudson's cause was Jodocus Hondius, whom Hudson knew when he was living in London. Hondius, now living in Amsterdam, was the leading map publisher in Holland. When Hudson did finally sign a contract, Hondius would serve as his interpreter in the negotiations, and sign as witness to Hudson's signature.

It was, however, politics and the king of France who finally convinced the VOC to employ Henry Hudson. Hearing that Hudson was in Amsterdam and not yet hired by the Dutch, King Henry IV of France asked his ambassador to Holland, Pierre Jeanin, to find out if Hudson was for hire. France wanted very much to share in the profitable Eastern trade and had hired other seamen to sail under the French flag.

Jeanin contacted Isaac Le Maire and asked him to speak to Hudson and to Plancius. Le Maire was an Amsterdam merchant who was a director of the Dutch East India Company, but was more interested in starting his own venture. Somehow, though Le Maire never directly asked Hudson to work for France, word leaked out to the directors of the VOC. Spurred on by the threat of competition, the company offered Hudson a contract. It was signed on January 8, 1609.

The Contract Is Signed

In the contract, the directors agreed to outfit a small sailing ship and provide it with men, provisions, and equipment. On this ship, "Hudson shall about the first of April, sail, in order to search for a passage by the North around the North side of Nova Zembla, and shall continue thus along that parallel until he shall be able to sail Southward to the latitude of sixty degrees."[4] The wording here shows that the directors clearly intended that Hudson should sail north, looking for the Northeast, not the Northwest Passage.

For these services, and for bringing back to the directors his knowledge of lands sighted and all his journals, logbooks, and charts, Hudson was to be paid eight hundred Dutch guilders. This was a very small amount, even for that time, but the deal was sweetened by two hundred more guilders to be paid to his wife if he were lost at sea, and promises of a larger reward if the passage were found. The contract also stipulated that if Hudson did find the passage, he would have to bring his wife and children to live in Holland and never work for anyone but the company ever again.

The contract clearly told Hudson the route he was to take—through the ice-clogged ocean above Novaya Zemlya. Perhaps word got to the directors that Hudson had twice before veered westward when ice blocked his ship, because an amendment to the contract was written just before he sailed telling Hudson: "To think of discovering no other route or passage, except the route around the north or northeast, above Nova Zembla [sic] . . . If it could not be accomplished at that time, another route would be subject of consideration for another voyage."[5]

Hudson agreed to the contract's terms. On March 25, 1609, Henry Hudson and sixteen crew members sailed north toward Norway. The *Half Moon* was flying the Dutch flag.

Chapter 7

Westward Ho!

Once again, Henry Hudson was heading north, traveling up the west coast of Norway on his way to find the Northeast Passage. He and his crew had to wonder whether this time would be successful. Did that ice-free passage that would take the new ship over the North Pole to Asia even exist? Henry Hudson himself no longer really believed it to be possible. However, in order to receive funding and support for his voyage of discovery, he needed to let his employers think that he thought it was.

Dealing With His Crew

It seems that on this trip, Hudson was not the only one on board the ship who quickly got tired of the ice, snow, fog, and stormy seas. The crew of the *Half Moon* was made up of both Dutch and English seamen.

On May 5, when the expedition reached North Cape, the northernmost point of Norway, the entries in the journal kept by mate Robert Juet mysteriously stopped until May 19. In fact, Juet had not recorded anything about the trip north, saying in his journal that "because it is a journey usually knowne, I omit reporting what passed."[1] By May 19, the *Half Moon* was heading west by north. Later that day, they headed east.

Hudson's logbooks and journals of this third voyage are missing, and in only a few places in the record kept by Juet does Hudson himself write. On Hudson's return to England after this voyage, the English authorities refused to let him travel to Amsterdam. Hudson entrusted his records to Emmanuel Van Meteren, the Dutch consul. Van Meteren then forwarded them to the directors of the Dutch East India Company. Van Meteren, a historian, published *Historie der Nederlanden,* a history of the Netherlands, in 1614. Since he was a historian who was careful about separating rumor from fact, his version of what happened from May 5 to May 19 has been trusted by other historians.[2]

Either from the journals or from a conversation with Henry Hudson, Van Meteren reported that a mutiny occurred aboard the *Half Moon.* The Dutch sailors had spent time sailing in the southern seas of the Indies. They were used to heat, not ice and cold. They refused to sail any farther north in the uncomfortable climate. First mate Robert Juet, who would figure heavily in later problems on Hudson's fourth voyage, is suspected by historians of being involved in the mutiny.[3]

Henry Hudson had already proven to be a captain who backed down under strong demands from his crew. This time, his willingness to compromise must have been increased by his own desire to sail west instead of north.[4] He had brought along all the charts necessary to travel either toward the Furious Overfall identified by Captain John Davis, or to go farther south along the North American coast toward Virginia and the Jamestown settlement. Captain John Smith, a prominent Jamestown settler, had supplied Hudson with charts suggesting that a Northwest Passage could be found just north of Jamestown.

Choosing the Route

According to Van Meteren, Hudson gave his crew a choice of the two westerly options. Historians differ as to which the crew chose, but it is known that Hudson wanted to cover both, starting at the south.[5] So, while the *Half Moon* retraced its sea miles toward Amsterdam from May 19 to May 25, on May 25, it turned decidedly west. By May 25, the men were in a storm again, near the Lofoten Islands off the coast of Norway. This drove their ship westward toward the Faeroe Islands, which lie between Iceland and Scotland.

The Faeroe Islands were inhabited by people who did some farming, lots of fishing, and raised sheep. They cultivated wool by pulling it from the roots directly off the live sheep's body.[6] The Faeroes are harsh, volcanic islands, with dramatic jagged rocks visible from the sea. On May 30, Hudson's crew walked on the land and filled caskets with fresh water for the trip west.

On June 15, a huge storm raged around them. The *Half Moon* lost its foremast, among other damage. The same storm forced a group of new colonists bound for Jamestown, Virginia, to seek harbor at Bermuda.

On the Coast of North America

The *Half Moon* reached the fishing banks off Newfoundland, now called the Grand Banks, on July 3. Here, Hudson's ship was among many French fishing boats that had fished these waters since the voyages of

American Indians view the Half Moon *as it approaches the coast of New Foundland.*

Source Document

A great many years ago, when men with a white skin had never yet been seen in this land, some Indians who were out a fishing, at a place where the sea widens, espied at some great distance something remarkably large floating on the water, and such as they had never seen before.

Some believed it to be an uncommonly large fish or animal, while others were of opinion it must be a very big house floating on the sea. At length the spectators concluded that this wonderful object was moving towards the land, and that it must be an animal or something else that had life in it; it would therefore be proper to inform all the Indians on the inhabited islands what they had seen, and put them on their guard. Accordingly they sent off a number of runners and watermen to carry the news to their scattered chiefs.[7]

Many years later, American Indians related the tale, passed down through the generations, of the local Indians' reaction to the first sighting of Hudson's Half Moon.

the Cabots. Traveling south, Hudson and his crew fished for cod, saw great schools of herring, and sighted land. Before they could anchor, however, a thick fog enveloped their ship. It lasted for three days, and when it finally cleared, they dropped anchor near Penobscot Bay in Maine.

The first visit from American Indians occurred on July 17. The Indians wanted to trade and they offered information about gold, silver, and copper mines that could be found to the northwest on shore. Other Indians came out in several canoes, but Hudson was wary of the strangers. The next day, the crew went on shore and cut down a tree to make the ship a new foremast. Then, on July 25, something strange happened.

According to Juet's journal, the twelve-man crew armed itself with muskets and other weapons and stole a canoe from the Indians. They also ransacked a village. They "drew the savages from their houses and robbed them, as they would have done to us."[8]

Of course, there was no proof that these Indians wished to rob the Europeans. Historian Llewelyn Powys, in discussing this shocking, but soon-to-be typical, way the Europeans treated the Indians, wrote, "That Hudson . . . should have consented to such an evil, is extraordinary, and can only confirm us in our belief that through some inherent weakness of character he was incapable of keeping his insubordinate crew under control."[9] Worse was yet to come.

The *Half Moon* headed south at 5:00 the next morning, towing the stolen Indian canoe, which eventually ended up splintered on jagged rocks. The ship continued sailing south until it reached the seas off the coast of Virginia. It is another mystery that Hudson, whose good friend Captain John Smith was in Jamestown, did

Source Document

When it shall please God to send you on the coast of Virginia, you shall do your best endeavour to find out a safe port in the entrance of some navigable river, making choice of such a one as runneth farthest into the land, and if you happen to discover divers portable rivers, and amongst them any one that hath two main branches, if the difference be not great, make choice of that which bendeth most toward the North-West for that way you shall soonest find the other sea. . . .

In all your passages you must have great care not to offen the naturals [natives], if you can eschew it; and imploy some few of your company to trade with them for corn and all other . . . victuals of you have any; and this you must do before they perceive you mean to plant among them; for not being sure how your own seed corn will prosper the first year, to avoid the danger of famine, use and endeavour to store yourselves of the country corn. . . .[10]

The instructions given to those starting the Virginia colony in 1606 gave explicit details as to where to settle and how to deal with the American Indians.

not stop at Jamestown harbor. Most probably it was because Hudson was sailing under the Dutch flag and had a crew half consisting of Dutch sailors.[11] Or perhaps, Hudson may have by then believed that the Northwest Passage, which Smith believed might lie just north of Jamestown, was definitely elsewhere.

Continuing south, the *Half Moon* turned north again before Cape Hatteras, off the coast of present-day North Carolina. By August 19, Hudson was sailing back the way he had come.

Robert Juet was very disturbed by the mood of the ship's cat, who "ranne crying from one side of the ship to the other, looking overboard. This made us wonder, but we saw nothing."[12] This worry is an example of the kind of superstition prevalent in the sixteenth and seventeenth centuries, even among some well-educated people of science. Cats were considered almost supernatural creatures, and their moods were watched for all kinds of predictions.[13]

Passing Chesapeake Bay on August 26, the ship reached Delaware Bay, and Cape May in present-day southern New Jersey. On September 2, the crew spotted present-day Navesink, New Jersey, and then Sandy Hook, New Jersey. By September 3, the ship's crew sailed past the south coast of Staten Island and saw the entrances to three large rivers. The decision to travel up the largest of these rivers would change Europe's view of the world.

Chapter 8

Feathers and Furs

Nearing the entrance to a river Hudson would call the River of the Mountains, the crew took soundings of the river's depth and anchored at five fathoms (one fathom is equal to six feet). By September 4, the men had spotted a better anchorage upstream, and they went ashore to fish. That afternoon, American Indians wearing deerskins visited the *Half Moon* and traded tobacco for knives and beads. Robert Juet praised the oak trees and the general countryside around him, and remarked on the corn and good bread made from it by the American Indians.

Encounter With the American Indians

One of the few remnants of Henry Hudson's own journal appeared at this point. Hudson described in detail the native people of the area and their customs. The entry is an example of his keen powers of observation. He remarked on the natives' clothing, food, and "their canoes, which are made of a single hollowed tree; their weapons are bows and arrows, pointed with sharp stones, which they fasten with hard resin."[1] Just who were these natives, whom the Europeans called Indians and who would figure so prominently in the *Half Moon*'s trip up the Hudson?

The American Indians who lived in the environs of the Hudson River were members of three separate language groups. When the *Half Moon* sailed up the river, the Mohicans (then called the Mahicanituk) controlled the east bank north of present-day Albany, New York, to the ocean, including parts of Long Island and east to Connecticut. On the west bank, the tribe ruled as far south as the present-day town of Catskill and west to Schenectady, New York.[2] The Mohawk people controlled lands farther west. To the south, the Lenni Lanape, or the Delaware, whose ruling tribe was the Minsis, controlled land south of the Mohawk all the way to the ocean and west "to and beyond the Delaware River."[3]

It was not until around 1630 that the Iroquois Confederacy, which included the Mohawk, Oneida, Onondaga, Cayuga, and Seneca, held sway in the vicinity of the river. The Iroquois became one of the three great American-Indian nations. Their enemies were the Mohican and the Lenni Lenape. By that time, Europeans were spread around the land. They figured highly in the divisions and conflicts between these native confederacies, by engaging one or the other of the American-Indian nations in struggles between conflicting European interests on the new continent. In 1609, none of the politics and warfare between the natives and the Europeans, which would eventually destroy all the Indian nations, could be foreseen by the inhabitants of this beautiful land. Nor could it have been foretold by the small band of seamen aboard the Dutch ship that sailed up the River of the Mountains.

By September 5, Hudson's crew members were exploring woods in what is now Monmouth County, New Jersey. These European seamen marveled at the tall, thick oaks and the linden trees. They helped themselves to berries that grew thick on vines. American-Indian families gathered around them, offering them tobacco. Robert Juet noted that Indians, "some dressed in cloaks of feathers, and others in furs," canoed out to the *Half Moon,* then anchored in Newark harbor.[4] Like all European visitors to this new world, Juet was looking for gold and other valuable metals. He remarked several times about the gleaming copper jewelry worn by the natives.

Exploration and the Loss of a Crewman

John Colman had been first mate on Hudson's 1607 voyage and was a valued crew member. He took the ship's boat with four sailors to explore a river twelve miles north of where the *Half Moon* was anchored. The men rowed through the Verrazano Narrows and saw what is now called New York Harbor. On their return, two canoes full of Indians attacked them, killing Colman with an arrow through his throat.

As night fell, the frightened survivors rowed back and forth in pelting rain. The tide was too strong for them to drop anchor. Finally, at 10:00 the next morning, they returned to the ship. Colman was buried at a place Hudson named Colman's Point, near Sandy Hook, New Jersey.

The belief among the Europeans that the American Indians were always ready to attack and steal grew even stronger after this incident. The next day, although they allowed Indians to come aboard the *Half Moon* to trade, they prominently displayed the bloodstained boat tied to the ship. They hoped an Indian would betray himself or others as the attackers, but no one showed signs of guilt.

When two large canoes of Indians appeared to trade and came aboard the ship on September 9, two of the natives were taken prisoner. The rest fled in surprise. Red coats were put on the two Indians and the crew made fun of them. Then the natives were imprisoned in the hold of the ship.

The Voyage Up the River

Sailing past Gull Island, now called Ellis Island, the *Half Moon* anchored near what is now Forty-second Street—though, of course, there was no New York City in 1607. They reached New York Harbor on September 11 and began their trip up the Hudson River. This river, which would be called the Mauritius

Source Document

Sept. 8.

Was very fair weather, we rode still very quietly. The people came aboard us, and brought tobacco and Indian wheat, to exchange for knives and beads, and offered us no violence. . . .

Sept. 9.

Fair weather. In the morning, two great canoes came aboard full of men; the one with their bows and arrows, and the other in show of buying knives to betray us; but we perceived their intent. We took two of them to have kept them and put red coats on them and would not suffer the other to come near us. So they went on land, and two others came abord in a canoe; we took the one and let the other go; but he which we had taken, got up and leaped over-board. Then we weighed and went off into the channel of the river, and anchored there all night.[5]

The journal of Robert Juet recalls the sometimes-tense relations between American Indians and Europeans.

Giovanni Verrazano explored the Hudson River in 1524, over eighty years before Henry Hudson. However, Verrazano only managed to venture about six miles up the river.

by the Dutch, was not actually discovered by Henry Hudson.

Giovanni da Verrazano first sailed into New York Harbor in 1524. This Italian navigator was sailing for France, and in a letter to King Francis I, he described "a very pleasant situation among some little steep hills, through which a very large river, deep at its mouth, forced its way to the sea."[6] Verrazano sent his ship's boat about six miles up this river, where his crew saw a land fertile and worthy of settlement. They also encountered many friendly natives. A stiff wind drove the boat back to the ship, and Verrazano pulled up his anchor and sailed away.

The next year, a Portuguese captain named Estevan Gomez, sailing for Spain, spotted this large river but did not sail into it. Gomez called the river the St. Antonio.

But Hudson's small ship, the *Half Moon,* did sail up the great river, anchoring the night of September 13 near the present-day site of Grant's Tomb. The next morning, the ship continued to sail up the river, thirty-six miles to near what is now West Point. Juet noted that the water was deep, the land grew high and mountainous, and the river was full of fish.[7]

Relations With the Indians

On September 15, the *Half Moon* sailed sixty miles through the Catskill Mountains. The two humiliated red-coated Indians climbed through a porthole and swam for shore, yelling angrily at the departing ship.

Hudson, Juet, and the crew continued to display a very mixed reaction to the natives of this land the Europeans wished to settle. Juet, later that same night, wrote, "We found a very loving people, with very old men, and we were well taken care of."[8] The American Indians continued to be friendly and gracious.

In another remnant of Hudson's own journal, he described a particularly pleasant encounter with the Indians: "I sailed to the shore in one of their canoes, with an old man, who was the chief of a tribe consisting of 40 men and 17 women." Hudson remarked on the solid construction of the natives' large house, and on the great quantity of corn laid out to dry, "enough to load three ships, besides what was growing in the fields." The Indians spread mats, sent men with bows and arrows after game, and "killed a fat dog, and skinned it in great haste with shells which they had got out of the water." The Indians invited Hudson to spend the night and were disappointed when he wanted to go back to his ship. Believing he might be afraid of them, they broke their arrows and "threw them in the fire" to prove their trustworthiness.[9] Hudson did not spend the night, but he did record the friendly encounter in his journal.

The American Indians of the area continued to be friendly and generous. They brought fruit and beaver and otter skins to trade for knives, hatchets, and beads. But by September 20, as the *Half Moon* traveled up the river, the ship entered narrow and shallow waters. The ship's boat, with five men, rowed six miles farther north. They discovered that the channel was very narrow but seemed to deepen again farther on.

The next day, there were so many American Indians swarming all around the ship, that Hudson decided to weigh anchor at an area that the natives called Schenectada. The ship's carpenter went ashore to make a foreyard (part of a mast). Meanwhile, Hudson and Juet decided to entertain some of the

Hudson found the American Indians of the Catskill Mountain area very friendly.

American-Indian chiefs with alcoholic drinks. The chiefs, totally unused to liquor, became very drunk, very quickly. One old man passed out cold. This frightened his companions, who left the ship and returned with wampum—beads of polished shell used as money—to lay beside their unconscious elder. When the chief awoke the next day, feeling fine, the Indians believed a curse had been lifted. They brought more gifts and wampum, and made speeches of thanks to Hudson.[10]

Disappointment

The ship's boat had continued upriver about twenty-five miles while these scenes were taking place. The crewmen found, to their disappointment, that the channel became too narrow and shallow for the boat to continue. It must have been a great disappointment for Hudson to have proof that this river, on which he had placed such hope, would never lead him to the Northwest Passage.

Reluctantly, on September 23, Henry Hudson turned the *Half Moon* south, retracing the miles down the great Hudson River. The crew took time to walk on the west bank, noting the wonderful trees, the good land for agriculture, and the stone for houses. On the trip south, relations between the seamen and the American Indians continued to be friendly until the ship reached the area below Peekskill, located midway between Albany and New York Harbor.

There, on October 1, while other Indians were trading skins for trinkets, one Indian leaped from a

This 1635 Dutch map shows the Noord River (Hudson River) and the various wildlife and American-Indian tribes surrounding it. The maker of this map drafted it in an odd way. North is toward the right side of the map, and West is toward the top.

canoe, entered Juet's cabin window, and stole a pillow, two shirts, and two belts to be worn across the chest for supporting cartridges, called bandoliers. A seaman shot the Indian in the chest and killed him. The rest of the Indians leaped for their canoes and even jumped into the water. One native tried to overturn the ship's boat, but the cook cut off one of his hands with a sword. The man drowned, and the *Half Moon* weighed anchor and sailed downriver for six miles before night fell.

At daybreak, American Indians began to chase the ship in canoes, shooting arrows. The crew fired muskets, and two or three natives were killed. Then, a group of about a hundred Indians was spotted at a point of land, with bows raised. This time, Juet shot a light cannon, killing two more Indians. The rest ran off into the woods. Still more canoes followed the ship, and still more Indians were killed. The American Indians were learning quickly about the superior firepower of these strange European visitors.

Finally, Hudson's ship arrived at a bay near an island the Indians called Manna-hata (present-day Manhattan). By October 4, the *Half Moon* had sailed out of the great river and entered open sea. Hudson and his men headed toward England. They arrived at Dartmouth on November 7, 1609.

Chapter 9

The Last Voyage

Why did Henry Hudson sail his Dutch ship into an English harbor? Once again, the answer lies in what is not said in Juet's journal. The Dutch sailors, who had mutinied during the northward-bound portion of the voyage, were probably not overeager to return to Holland and face possible punishment. A Dutch mate, according to historian Llewelyn Powys, thought the ship should winter in Newfoundland. The reasoning was that they would be near the Furious Overfall, and could continue the search for the Northwest Passage the next spring.[1] Hudson suggested that they spend the winter in Ireland, but it is possible that the English crew insisted on returning to England at once.[2] In addition, since he had broken the terms of his contract by heading west, Hudson himself might have been reluctant to return to Holland.

Problems at Home

Whatever the reasons, once in England, Hudson lost no time in contacting the directors of the Dutch East India Company. He told them that as soon as he had been paid for this voyage, he was willing to head west again to search farther north for the fabled Northwest Passage. He would leave early in March and catch whale and fish so that, whether he found the Northwest Passage or not, he could bring back a profit for his employers. He also requested that six or seven of his crewmen be replaced with less insubordinate sailors.

None of his requests, however, would be met. The English government refused to let Hudson or the English members of his crew leave England. Hudson was accused of working against the good of his own country.[3] Rumors of Hudson's having discovered a great river surrounded by highly desirable land had reached English ears. The boasts of the returning seamen around the ports probably magnified their adventures, as well.

By the time Hudson's message reached Holland and the Dutch East India Company, Hudson was under virtual house arrest in England. His employer's instructions, delivered in January 1610, were that Hudson should return at once to Amsterdam. Hudson's Dutch contact, Emanuel Van Meteren, was quietly angry at the high-handed way England had dealt with the returning sailors. "Many persons thought it rather unfair that these sailors should have been prevented from laying their accounts and reports before their employers," was all Van Meteren would allow himself to say.[4]

The *Half Moon* and some of its Dutch sailors finally returned to Amsterdam in July of 1611. Meanwhile, Van Meteren sent Hudson's charts and journals to Holland. (Most of those writings of Hudson's were reported on in various publications of the period but have now been lost.)

Looking for a Sponsor

Hudson had attempted to find a Northeast Passage, funded by the Muscovy Company, through the frozen waters above Novaya Zemlya—and failed. He had been hired by the Dutch to find a Northeast Passage in the same waters—and had not even looked. He had failed to find a Northwest Passage along the coast of North America and by sailing one hundred and fifty miles up a large river. However, the northern route through the Furious Overfall remained to be explored. Would anyone hire him to do so?

Several wealthy London merchants, such as Sir Thomas Smythe, Sir Dudley Digges, and Master John Wolstenholme, led other influential merchants to fund a plan to do just that. Prince Henry, son of the English King James I, also supported the outfitting of a ship called the *Discovery,* which left London on April 17, 1610. Henry Hudson was its captain.

Where Hudson Headed and Why

Information about what Hudson may have presented to his next employers came from several sources. This information was likely inaccurate, as navigation, in the sixteenth and seventeenth centuries, was still more of an art than a science. Cartographers had to put together the information for their maps from the conflicting charts and journals of various navigators' voyages.

Hudson's knowledge of the northwest Arctic region came from these flawed maps. He also took information from journals, logbooks, and charts compiled by other English explorers. One of these was Martin Frobisher, who had sailed north of Labrador, to the north of Canada, in 1576. Frobisher believed that North America was connected to Asia through the Arctic. The Northwest Passage, he hoped, lay in a large bay or strait above North America. Frobisher named this passage "Frobishers Straightes." Even though ice blocked his ship one hundred fifty miles inland, he believed he had found the Northwest Passage.

Having found some black stone that seemed to contain gold ore, Frobisher was able to receive funding from Queen Elizabeth I of England for a second voyage. This second voyage was taken up much more with mining for gold—which proved to be what is called fool's gold and worthless—than with searching for the Northwest Passage.

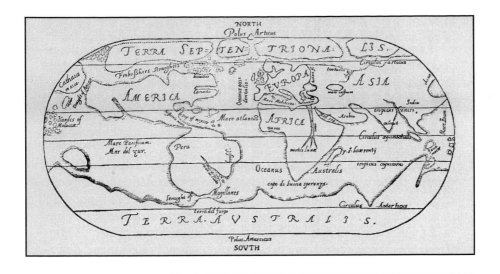

Martin Frobisher depicted the Northwest Passage as "Frobishers Straightes" in his 1578 map. According to Frobisher's map, after navigating the "Straightes," a vessel would just need to sail down the "Straight of Anian" to reach the Pacific Ocean.

Although the Northwest Passage was not found on either of Frobisher's voyages, George Best, a passenger on the second voyage, published a world map that showed Frobishers Straightes across the top of Canada, entering the Pacific Ocean at what he called the Straight of Anian. This map was an improvement on Gerardis Mercator's map of 1569, in that Greenland was finally placed in the correct spot. However, this map also showed islands that simply do not exist.

Explorer John Davis sailed on three separate trips to the northern Arctic, originating the term "Furious Overfall." On his first voyage in 1585, mistaking Greenland for an undiscovered land, he sailed his ship up an inlet that led him one hundred eighty miles west through Greenland. Bad weather made him leave the exploration of what he called Cumberland Sound for his second voyage.

During this second voyage, Davis discovered two new straits on the Labrador coast, which he called Davis Inlet and Hamilton Inlet. Although he found no through passage, he convinced his backers that it would take just one more try. He wanted to explore the northern part of Davis Strait. He sailed within 356 miles of the Arctic Circle in this body of water now called Baffin Bay. The usual culprits—ice and icebergs—turned him east, just as he believed he had spotted a clear and open sea beyond the ice—which did not exist.

Davis turned his ship south, passing Cumberland Strait and Frobisher's Strait (modern spelling), which he called Lumley's Inlet. The Furious Overfall, which is actually water rushing into Hudson Strait out of Hudson Bay, was next to greet the ship. Davis remarked in his journal, "to our great admiration, we saw the sea falling down into the gulfe with a mighty overfall and roaring, and with divers[e] circular motions like whirlpools."[5] Davis believed that crossing this inlet would lead him to the Northwest Passage.

Davis's journals, published by Richard Hakluyt, were studied by Henry Hudson as he prepared for his voyages west. The Molyneux Globe, made public in 1592—the first globe made in England—incorporated Davis's charts. In 1599, an accompanying map, the

Wright-Molyneux map of the world, was also available to Hudson.

The globe, while appearing accurate, has no northern boundary. The Great Lakes are one large body emptying into nothing, and the latitudes of straits, inlets, and islands are generally inaccurate. Names of islands and straits came from various voyages where navigators renamed what had already been discovered, usually after themselves. Greenland, as usual, was a problem. According to author and cartographer Donald Johnson, "some remarkable changes were made to Greenland's geography" on the Molyneux Globe.[6] It must have been very difficult for a seventeenth-century mapmaker who had to come up with a compromise between different voyages with differing chunks of land appearing on conflicting charts.

The next navigator to follow Davis into the frozen northwest was George Weymouth, in 1602. He hoped to be able to sail far enough inland to find the open sea Davis had written about, but was not able to gain entry. His crew, encountering terrible ice, refused to keep going north or to spend the winter in the bleak landscape. So Weymouth turned south and sailed into Hudson Strait from the north. He made one more voyage, in 1605.

Hudson had Weymouth's logbook and journal from both trips. When Henry Hudson sailed from England on April 7, 1610, he was armed with information—and disinformation—and George Weymouth's boat, the *Discovery*. This time, Hudson was headed west—and north—on an open quest for the Northwest Passage.

Heading for the Furious Overfall

The *Discovery* was a larger ship than the *Hopewell* or the *Half Moon*. It left port with twenty-two crew members, several of whom were not experienced seamen. One of these individuals was Abacuk Prickett, a former hatmaker. Prickett would later provide the most detailed—and self-serving—surviving account of the voyage.

Some things were not very different on this voyage, however. Five of the crew members, one of them Hudson's son John, had been to sea with Henry Hudson before. Unfortunately, and somewhat mysteriously, considering his part in previous mutinous behavior aboard Hudson's ships, one of these men was Robert Juet, first mate. From Juet's logbooks, it is obvious that he was a very knowledgeable navigator. This may be why Hudson chose to ignore Juet's surly, resentful personality.

Another crew member, Master Coleburne, or Colbert, was hired as an advisor by the Merchant Adventurers, Hudson's employers for this voyage. Coleburne was set ashore even before the Discovery left England. Farther down the Thames River Hudson welcomed on board a man named Henry Greene in Coleburne's place. This was another odd and ultimately tragic decision.

Greene was not an experienced seaman, but he was certainly an experienced troublemaker. He was known around the docks as a seedy character who associated with dishonest people.[7] The first hint of trouble came as early as mid-May, when Hudson's ship was anchored off Iceland. Greene quarreled with the ship's surgeon, Edward Wilson, and insisted on fighting him on shore. Hudson defended Greene, saying that Wilson had a sharp tongue. It was not until the ship had left Iceland that Hudson became aware that Juet had told crew members that Greene was put on board as a stool pigeon, to "crack the credit" of mutinous actions by seamen.[8] Hudson was furious. He considered going back to Iceland and leaving Juet to find his way home on an English fishing boat. However, he did not. Once again, Hudson's lack of decisive leadership at crucial moments made him back down and continue on.

Because there was ice close to shore, the *Discovery* never anchored near Greenland. The crew continued to see vast icebergs as they passed Resolution Island and entered Hudson Strait, or the Furious Overfall. Attempting to go through the strait on June 25, Hudson was several weeks too early to find clear passage. The four hundred fifty-mile-long strait, one hundred miles wide, was still filled with ice that moved back and forth with the tides. The ship's compass became unreliable due to their nearness to the magnetic Pole, and Hudson could not move directly west.

The icy backdrop for this portrait of Henry Hudson was an all-too-familiar scene for the explorer.

He sailed south, turned north along the coast of Labrador, then turned south again because of ice.

On July 19, the ship came upon an island that Hudson named Cape Hold with Hope. He found the waters between this island and the mainland to be deep, and he sailed west along the southern shore of the strait. Since what has survived of Hudson's journal ends on August 3, the "various adventures encountered during these long weeks have been admirably described by Prickett," according to Llewelyn Powys.[9]

Finding a Passage?

At one point, the *Discovery* became completely enclosed with ice. Hudson had already gone three hundred miles farther into the strait than any navigator before him. He brought out his charts and let the men choose whether or not to go further. "One man . . . told the master that if he had 100 pounds, he would give 90 of it to be at home. . . . ," according to Prickett.[10] However, all the wishing could not stop the fact that much work would have to be done to turn the ship around and edge their way out of the ice. Finally, the ship was in a clear sea, sailing north and northwest. The men saw snow-covered, mountainous land to the southwest. Hudson called it "Desire Provoketh."[11]

The ship anchored near a large piece of ice, and the crew got out to stretch and fill casks with fresh water. A polar bear was spotted sitting on a single piece of ice, but when the ship's boat tried to approach it, the bear moved quickly away. Further northwest, the men spotted another bear, who jumped from one ice floe to another, as if intending to board the ship. Noticing the men lined up looking at it, the bear "Put her head between her hind legs and dived under the ice, moving from one piece to another until she was out of our reach."[12]

Finally, the ice seemed to be behind them. The ship entered a narrow channel between Cape Digge and Cape Wolstenholme. Hudson believed that, at last, he had found the Northwest Passage. Open sea was ahead of the ship as Hudson recorded the last remaining entry in his journal. Prickett, Greene, and a few others went by boat to Digge's Island, where they found deer, streams, green grass, and stone bird traps that showed humans had lived here before.

The seamen wanted to stay a few days on the island and explore further, but Hudson insisted that they move onward. He navigated the ship south, eager to continue exploring what he hoped was the Northwest Passage. The ship passed several groups of islands along the eastern coast of Smith Island. Hudson steered past Cape Jones and entered James Bay. There, things began to fall apart.

A Trial Aboard Ship

For several weeks, the *Discovery* sailed back and forth in this large bay. The men began to murmur and then talk openly about their dissatisfaction with the apparent aimlessness of the voyage. Hudson was frustrated and accused Juet of being disloyal. Juet responded by asking for a trial in front of the whole crew.

On September 10, a trial was held that clearly placed blame on Juet for inciting past trouble among the crew, including urging the men to keep "muskets charged and swords ready in their cabins, for they would be used before the voyage was over."[13] For once, Hudson had the crew on his side. After the trial, he demoted Juet from first mate and replaced him with Robert Bylot. Several other loyal crewmen replaced troublemakers as officers. Hudson promised the demoted men that if they behaved well from that point on, he would forget their insubordinate behavior. For the moment, the grumbling stopped.

Hudson continued to roam around James Bay with a ship full of puzzled seamen, who began to think he was lost. Several times he started out when seas were too rough, and once, despite a warning by Philip Staffe, the ship's carpenter, the ship was stranded on a rock for twelve hours. Not usually a man to show anger, this time Hudson went back and forth not only in James Bay, but in his handling of the men. He alternated threats of hanging for mutinous behavior with assurances that he would be lenient if good behavior continued for the rest of the journey. Time—and good weather—were beginning to run out.

All the wandering in James Bay meant that the *Discovery* and its crew would have to find a place to spend the winter. On November 1, having dropped anchor in Rupert's Bay in the shadow of a four hundred-foot-high granite hill, the *Discovery* was hauled close to shore. "By the tenth of the month the *Discovery* was frozen in," wrote historian Llewelyn Powys.[14]

It is not hard to imagine how this tired bunch of sailors felt about the prospect of spending a winter in a frozen wilderness. Not only were they unaware of exactly where they were, but no one was getting along. And yet, their ship frozen into the ice, there was no other choice. How would the crew, and Hudson himself, deal with the harsh winter?

Chapter 10

Mutiny in a Winter Wonderland

There could not have been a more thoroughly inhospitable place to spend the winter than the area beneath a mountainous outcropping of rock on the shore of James Bay. James Bay is a U-shaped extension at the southeastern corner of Hudson Bay. Its coastline includes part of the present-day Canadian provinces of Quebec and Ontario. Though Inuit peoples have lived in this bleak and difficult land for centuries, it is not a place that Europeans of the seventeenth century—or today—would go. A tremendously difficult winter was about to begin.

Although there were still food supplies on the ship, there was not enough food to last twenty-two men through the winter. Birds had been seen nesting in the hills along the shore, and Hudson offered rewards to any man who brought back a bird or animal for the crew to eat. No man was allowed to hunt alone. There had to be two—one with a musket and one with a pike—a sharp instrument to finish animals off, since musket fire was inaccurate. Provisions were distributed carefully.

Preparing for the Winter

Hudson decided to build a house on land, even though he had turned the idea down earlier. Philip Staffe, the carpenter, objected strongly to this idea. It was too cold. The boards would freeze to the ground and the nails could easily freeze to his lips and tear the skin off—carpenters hold extra nails between their lips as they are hammering. Hudson lashed out at Staffe, threatening to hang him.[1] Though the house was finally built, an incident that altered the course of the voyage occurred the day after Hudson lost his temper with Staffe.

The day after his confrontation with Hudson, Staffe took his gun to hunt for birds. Henry Greene went along. Earlier that month, the gunner, John Williams, had died. It was the custom at the time that any possessions of a deceased seaman would be sold to the highest bidder. Henry Greene, who had come on board with less clothing and fewer provisions than the other seamen, told Hudson he would pay top price for Williams's things when he returned to England. Hudson, therefore, awarded Greene the homespun wool gown Williams had worn, to the irritation of the rest of the crew.

When Greene went hunting with Staffe, who had had a conflict with his captain, Hudson took this as an act of disloyalty from Greene. Hudson took away Greene's newly acquired gown and awarded it to his new first mate, Robert Bylot. When Greene objected, Hudson attacked Greene's character and threatened not to pay him if he did not improve his behavior.

This incident, magnified by the stress of the approaching winter, turned Greene totally against Hudson. Indeed, more than anything else, it set in motion a wish for revenge that would end in tragedy. In the meantime, the men had to find a way to survive the winter.

In the early months of the winter, there was an abundance of birds stopping on their way south, and fish could be caught through holes in the ice. In later months, the crew had to scour the hills in search of anything edible, including moss and frogs, and a substance made from a tree bud, which eased aches and pains. What the men did not have were growing plants. Without the vitamin C contained in vegetables and fruits, people can get a disease called scurvy. This terrible disease causes the gums to rot and the arms and legs to swell. To make matters worse, frostbite was ever present. The monotony of the frozen landscape must have caused a terrifying depression, a hopelessness in these luckless sailors.

Thawing Out

Finally, as spring approached, the ice in the bay began to crack. An American Indian appeared at the ship, and Hudson bargained with him, calling for private stores of knives and hatchets from his crew to barter with. It is a sign of the disrespect the crew held for Hudson that only Hudson, John King, and Prickett offered personal items for bartering. The Indian came back with deerskins and beaver skins and told Hudson in sign language that there were people in the surrounding hills. Although he indicated he would return, he did not.

As the ice began to break, fishing from the boat began. The first day out they caught five hundred fish. On other days there were not so many. Prickett reported in his journal that Greene and seaman Wilson plotted to take the net and the ship's boat and set out for themselves.[2] But Hudson had taken the large ship's boat, which had a sail and was called a shallop, to explore the woods where he had seen smoke. He hoped to meet with American Indians who would supply the crew with meat.

Though Hudson was gone for several days, he had given instructions that the *Discovery* should be made ready for sailing on his return. During his trip, he was unable to find any natives. Historians consider it rather odd that a captain would take off on a boat, leaving his crew to fend for themselves, after such a difficult winter.[3] Hudson returned discouraged and for some unexplained reason, removed Bylot from his position as first mate and replaced him with John King. This latest first mate could neither read nor write, which further pushed Bylot toward Greene and Juet, already planning mutiny. It was under these conditions that Henry Hudson and his crew prepared to leave James Bay.

Mutiny!

As the *Discovery* sailed out of its winter harbor, Hudson divided first the remaining bread and then the cheese. According to Prickett, "The remaining cheese was equally divided by the master, although he was cautioned otherwise, for there were some men who were unable to ration themselves, quickly eating all that was given them."[4] This proved true. Greene ate a whole week's worth of bread in three days; William Wilson ate two week's worth of bread in one day, and made himself sick. The expression "character is destiny" would prove all too true for Greene and Wilson.

As the food problems continued, the ship was sailing northwest. By June 18, the men were once more sailing through ice. Hudson demanded that Nicholas Simmes, the ship's boy, open each seaman's personal sea chest and bring him any loaves of bread the men might have stolen and hoarded. Thirty loaves of bread were delivered. Even faced with this blatant theft, Hudson did not act decisively. Prickett wondered "why he did not stop the offense right at the beginning, but let it grow to the extent that it would overthrow himself and many other honest men."[5]

Once again, the *Discovery* was marooned in ice. Now, food was running out. Rumors spread that Hudson had plenty of bread and cheese and aquavit (a liquor) hidden in his cabin to feed himself and his favorites. Hudson, rather than rallying his crew, withdrew, "not caring to goe one way or other."[6]

Did Hudson favor certain crew members? Did he save food for himself and his favorites? Greene and William Wilson, encouraged by Juet, believed it. They also believed that Hudson, once the ship was freed from the ice, would try again to find the Northwest Passage, despite the desperate food situation.

Prickett had been left lame by frostbite during the harsh winter spent in James Bay. He was lying in his bunk on Saturday, June 21, when Greene and William Wilson entered his cabin. They told him about their plan to put Hudson and all sick men into the shallop and set them adrift. Prickett, in his journal, professed alarm at this plan. Mutiny was the worst offense possible: If caught, the culprits could be hanged. He also said that he would "stay with the ship, but did not want to hurt myself and others by being involved in such a deed."[7]

Greene told Prickett that he would be placed in the shallop if he did not go along with their plan. Prickett recorded that he said, "then the will of God be done."[8] Prickett tried to talk with William Wilson after Greene stormed out of his cabin. Wilson believed there was no other solution, that they must act immediately to retain their credibility. Prickett claimed to have asked the mutineers to take time, to let him talk with Hudson. The mutineers refused to hear of it. Prickett spoke to Juet and to other men involved in the mutiny. Prickett asked them to take an oath that they would not harm any man, and that what they were doing they fully believed was best for the larger part of the crew.

The oath backfired. It had the effect of solidifying the mutineers' purpose. When asked who would be put into the shallop and set adrift, Greene told Prickett that it would be Hudson and anyone who was sick, plus Philip Staffe and John King. The reasoning was that Hudson favored those two men and gave them extra food.

All through the long night, Prickett tried to talk the mutineers out of their plan, or at least into executing it without bloodshed. Henry Greene kept watch over the sleeping Henry Hudson. Greene wanted to be sure that Hudson would not wake up too soon, realize what was going on, and rally other crew members to put down the mutiny. Although Prickett was able to talk the mutineers out of putting Staffe in the shallop, Greene insisted that he be watched closely so that he would not alert Hudson. Bylot and William Wilson made sure that both Staffe and King were sleeping soundly.

As the sun was about to rise, Mathues, the cook, who was in on the mutiny, began to prepare breakfast as usual. The sound of water being drawn for the kettle was the signal agreed on by the mutineers to begin. Greene and another seaman started talking with the carpenter, Philip Staffe, who had slept on the deck of the ship, hoping to divert his attention until they had Hudson safely tied up. John King was called into the hold and bolted in. When Hudson came out of his cabin, John Thomas and the cook seized him. Before Hudson had time to pull free, William Wilson threw a rope around him, binding his arms.

Prickett struggled to the door of his cabin, begging the mutineers to be merciful. He was told to go back in his cabin, but he had seen the sick men dragged from their cabins and forced into the readied shallop. Philip Staffe, the carpenter, asked the mutineers if they knew they would all be hanged for their crime when they reached England. Though he had not been forced to get into the shallop, he said he would not stay on the ship unless they made him. He was told to go. He did, first asking for his chest full of carpenter's tools to be put into the shallop. Prickett urged him to stay. He hoped the carpenter could make the mutineers less violent, but Staffe replied that it was now too late for him to stay.

Set Adrift

Staffe believed, as Hudson did, that no man on the *Discovery* had the ability to sail the ship back to England. He asked Prickett to leave signs at the capes where they anchored to indicate that they had been

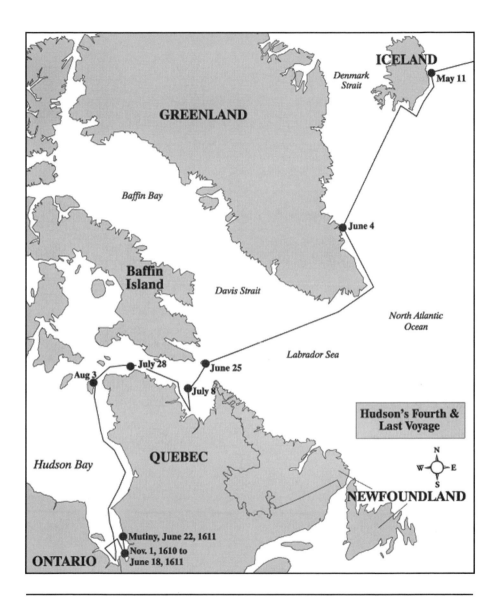

Henry Hudson's fourth voyage through the Hudson Bay abruptly ended in mutiny.

there. Those in the shallop had already planned to follow the *Discovery.*

By now, Hudson and his young son John were in the shallop, along with Staffe, Lodlo, Woodhouse, Moore, Faner, King, and Bute. The carpenter managed to talk Greene into allowing the men in the shallop a gun with powder and shot, a few spears, and an iron pot with a small amount of grain. All the time the shallop was being readied to be set adrift, the seamen still on board ship set about looting the cabins and the sea chests within.

The *Discovery* sailed into the wind and out of the ice with the shallop attached. When they were almost clear of the ice, the shallop was cut loose. The ship, under full sail, headed west. Prickett reported that there was an immediate search for food, and though they found extra provisions in Hudson's cabin, it was no more than any careful captain would store. The mutineers were so busy ransacking for food that they had not noticed the shallop following them. "They noticed now that the shallop had come into sight, so they set the mainsail and topsails, and flew away as though from an enemy," wrote Prickett.[9] The shallop was left far behind. It was never seen again.

Spears and Starvation

The three men who had headed the mutiny and now were in charge of the crew of the *Discovery,* Henry Greene, William Wilson, and Robert Juet, were the least disciplined, most negative, and nastiest

This painting, entitled Last Voyage of Henry Hudson, *was painted by John Collier in 1881. It depicts Hudson with his son, drifting aimlessly after falling victim to the mutiny on the* Discovery.

troublemakers aboard the ship. Prickett, whose account of the mutiny and the trip back to England paints him in the best possible colors, seems to have been the only rational person aboard. Greene evidently thought so, or else he thought Prickett would make a good scapegoat. Shortly after losing sight of the shallop for the last time, Greene asked Prickett to stay in the master's—Henry Hudson's—cabin and take charge. When Prickett protested that "Robert Juet was more fit for the job," Greene answered that Juet was not to enter the master's cabin or deal with the charts and journals.[10] Distrust of each other was strong among this crew of mutineers.

Prickett was also put in charge of handing out bread, and was soon accused of stealing what Greene himself had stolen from the storage area. According to Llewelyn Powys, "the mutineers had spared Prickett's life for no other reason than that they felt confidence in his power of presenting the authorities with a plausible and well-contrived story when they should reach England."[11] Bylot kept his own logbook, which would prove useful to him in later years. It became clear almost immediately that no one on board had any real idea of where they were going.

Finally, at the end of July, when the crew had been surviving on a few birds and a harsh grass called cockle-grass, they saw Cape Digges and Cape Wolstenhome, at the southern entrance to Hudson Strait. After being stranded on a rock overnight, they were released by a westward-flowing current. The boat went ashore and the men killed thirty birds. The next day, July 28, as the ship was rounding a point of land, the men saw about fifty Inuits in canoes, rowing toward them. Both the Europeans and the Inuits were startled, excited, and wary.

To allay suspicion, an exchange of "hostages" took place. One European seaman went to an Inuit tent, and one native remained on the sailors' boat. The Inuits offered presents of skins, furs, and walrus teeth to the Europeans. Prickett described the natives as "bigge-boned, broad-faced, flat-nosed and small-footed, like the Tartars [natives of far-eastern Russia]."[12]

Cooking was primitive aboard ships in Hudson's day.

The next day proved vastly different. The ship went back in to shore, with the lame Prickett remaining in the boat. That day, Henry Greene, William Wilson, John Thomas, Michael Perse, and Adrian Motter carried trade items to barter with the Inuits for meat and skins.

Prickett, in the small ship's boat, was startled by an unwelcome visitor. An Inuit climbed into the boat, and when Prickett motioned to him to leave, the Inuit pretended at first that he did not understand but started back to shore. Then Prickett saw a leg and an arm coming over the back of the boat. An arm was raised over Prickett's head and a knife came down on him just as he raised his right arm, deflecting the blade. The Inuit struck twice more. Prickett, though lame in the legs, was strong and muscular. He managed to grab the assailant's knife and reach for the small blade he kept on his own belt. He drove his blade through the throat of the attacking native, only then noticing that the same type of violence was going on ashore.

John Thomas and William Wilson had blades run through their intestines. Michael Perse and Henry Greene, wounded, fell into the boat. Adrian Motter, who had gone up to some rocks to search for a plant called sorrel, hurled himself down from the rocks and through the water toward the boat. The Inuits were swarming around the boat as Motter clung to its stern. Finally, Prickett, who was wounded in the thigh, got the boat clear of shore, and pulled Motter out of the water. Now the Inuits shot arrows as Motter and Perse rowed away. Greene was killed and Perse and Prickett wounded. The Inuits ran for their own boats. The *Discovery* was hidden from the rocky cove so there was no way of letting Bylot and Juet, still on the ship, know of their plight.

Finally, the boat was spotted. Everyone but Greene, who was unceremoniously dumped into the sea, were hauled aboard the ship. Within three days, William Wilson, Thomas, and Perse were all dead. Of the original crew, two of the chief instigators of the mutiny were dead, and only nine men were left on board the *Discovery*.

By the time the ship docked in Plymouth, England, and sailed up the River Thames, Juet had died of starvation. The rest of the men, surviving by eating seaweed, were too weak to stand up. Still alive, and unsure what would happen to them next, were Bylot, Prickett, Edward Wilson, Clemens, Mathues, Bond, Motter, and the ship's boy, Nicholas Syms.

Acquittal

What happened to these men who had set Captain Henry Hudson, his young son, and six other men adrift in the icy, turbulent waters of the far northern ocean? The answer is nothing. Even before a long-delayed trial, held in 1618, during which all parties were acquitted, Robert Bylot had been pardoned out of gratitude for his feat of bringing the *Discovery* home as captain. The truth was, the possibility that Hudson had found the Northwest Passage was worth more to the English merchants than the jailing or hanging of a few selfish mutineers. Everyone involved in the mutiny was careful to say that it was imminent starvation that caused them to place Hudson, whom they blamed for hoarding provisions, and sick men who were unable to work in the shallop. To say he was incompetent would almost certainly have had them hanged.[13] Instead, they made Hudson sound like a thief. They also asserted that no one was harmed in any way when they were shoved into the shallop.

On July 27, 1612, Bylot, Edward Wilson, and Prickett became members of a company of merchants chartered by King James I. "The Discoverers of the North-west Passage" as the company was called, sent out the *Discovery* along with the *Resolution,* with Prickett and Bylot as passengers. Although the ships' official goal was to rescue Hudson and the rest of the men, the real purpose was to find the Northwest Passage they believed existed, which would take them to Asia. This passage, they believed, would occur somewhere at the western shore of Hudson Bay. However, no strait was found. In 1616 Robert Bylot captained the *Discovery* once again and searched Baffin Bay. Though he explored and mapped the entire bay, and went three hundred miles farther north than Davis had sailed, Bylot was finally convinced that "there was no passage, no hope of a passage."[14] No mention was made of the supposed search for Henry Hudson and his luckless sailors.

The Legacy

Henry Hudson and his fellow occupants of the shallop were never heard from again. Rumors of the sighting of a ruined house on the shores of James Bay, built in the English fashion, came back to England over the years. A fur trapper, Pierre Esprit Radisson, recorded in his diary that he found an old house demolished and bullet-riddled. Captain Zachariah Gillam, in a memo from the Hudson's Bay Company, recorded that the company's first factory, Fort Charles on James Bay, was constructed "upon the ruins of a house which had been built there above 60 years before by the English."[1] A Captain James, wintering with his crew on Charlton Island in 1631–1632, discovered a row of thick stakes driven into the ground, obviously sharpened by an ax that might have been Philip Staffe's. If these stories are true, then Hudson's shallop at least reached land and the men attempted to survive. What happened to them next will probably never be known.

Hudson's wife was left very poor after her husband and son's disappearance. Katherine Hudson repeatedly petitioned the government for relief. She finally received money to outfit one of her other sons, Richard, to take a position in the British East India Company. Richard did well in his career. Katherine Hudson traveled to India and became wealthy in the import-export business, which was highly unusual for a woman of her day.[2]

A Geographical Legacy

Beyond the personal, Henry Hudson's legacy is immense. We now know his name chiefly through the

Henry Hudson's exploration would pave the way for the Dutch Colony of New Amsterdam (present-day New York City).

Source Document

1. We consent that the States-General or West India Company shall freely enjoy all farms and houses . . . and that within six months they shall have free liberty to transport all such arms and ammunition as now do belong to them, or else they shall be paid for them. . . .

6. It is consented to, that any people may freely come from the Netherlands and plant in this country, and that Dutch vessels may freely come hither, and any of the Dutch may freely return home, or send any sort of merchandise home in vessels of their own country. . . .

18. If it does appear that the West India Company of Amsterdam do really owe any sums of money to any persons here, it is agreed that recognition and other duties payable by ships going for the Netherlands be continued for six months longer. . . .[3]

This document was written when former Dutch territory in the New World was taken over by the British in 1664. It outlined the rights Dutch inhabitants would enjoy under English rule.

places and things named for him: Hudson River, Hudson Strait, and Hudson Bay, and the Hudson Bay Company, chartered in 1670 by the British. In addition, the Hudson River valley; Hudson, New York; and the Hudson school of painters—and many other places and entities that have taken his name— keep Hudson always in the public eye.

Because of his navigation of the Hudson River, the Dutch were able to lay claim and to colonize North America in Delaware and Connecticut. Dutch dominance lasted until the English duke of York drove the Dutch from the Hudson River valley in 1664. However, the Dutch remained influential for another century in New York, Connecticut, New Jersey, Pennsylvania, and Delaware.

The entire development of the Hudson River valley is due to Hudson's explorations up what he called the Great River of the Mountains. On the plus side, it brought European settlers to this new land. Sadly, however, it began the destruction of the tribes and lives of the Mohawk, Mohican, Lenni Lenape, and all Indians of the Iroquois nation.

Hudson's exploration of the Arctic Ocean, particularly the northwest above Canada, helped lead to the formation of the British Hudson Bay Company, chartered in 1670 after the English had driven out the Dutch. The English then held a monopoly to trade furs in all the territory drained by rivers that flowed into Hudson Bay. This company was unique in its organization and self-sufficiency.[4]

Again, this commercial success was not kind to the Indians of the area. Around Hudson Bay, the lands had been controlled by the Inuit to the northeast; the Cree, an Algonquian people, to the east; and the Chippewa to the west. It is among these Indians that Hudson and the survivors of the shallop may have lived, for however long.

Henry Hudson did not find the Northwest Passage, nor did he complete his earlier goal of finding a Northeast Passage. Not until the twentieth century would the Northwest Passage—which requires ice-cutting ships—be crossed. Although other explorers had ranged northward, only Hudson explored the entire Arctic. He went as far as the continuous ice would let him. He showed future explorers what were, and were not, navigable waters. A conflicted man, Hudson paid dearly for the fatal flaw of failing to exercise his authority appropriately. People of vision often are single-minded, caring more for their passion—be it discovery, geography, or science, or something else— than they do for individuals. Henry Hudson was such a person.

The *Half Moon* Today

The story of Henry Hudson, particularly his discovery that led to European settlement of the Hudson River, has long intrigued Americans interested in sailing. As early as 1909 Holland built a replica of the *Half Moon*. This ship was given to the United States for a celebration of both Henry Hudson and Robert Fulton, the man

A flag flies from the mast of a reproduction of the Half Moon.

who first operated steamboats with commercial success. This replica was shipped to the United States aboard a larger ship, but sailed around New York Harbor and the Hudson River. Historian Donald Johnson remarked that at one time, part of the *Half Moon's* bowsprit was torn out when it collided with the reproduction of Fulton's *Clermont*, built to commemorate the one hundredth anniversary in 1909 of the *Clermont's* trip from New York to Albany in record time.[5] Sailors carved pieces of the damaged bowsprit into reproductions of the ship and sold them as souvenirs.

On June 10, 1989, a new and more accurate reproduction of the *Half Moon* was launched, near Albany, New York. This ship, which takes part in tall ship displays and docks frequently in Albany, New York; Hoboken, New Jersey; and other ports along the Hudson River, can be visited by individuals and school groups. Currently, the *Half Moon* takes middle school classes on as crew and teaches them about sailing and history. Although some building elements are different from the original, to cut costs, many original materials were used, such as oak, pine, and fir. Henry Hudson, obsessed with finding the Northwest Passage, might be puzzled that what interests people now is the *means* to the end he never found. For him, the *Half Moon* was an ordinary, necessary, and rather confining ship. Today, its replica is a living history lesson.

Timeline

1582—Richard Hakluyt publishes *Diverse Voyages,* in which he discusses a possible Northwest Passage.

1587—Captain John Davis sails west across the Atlantic and finds and names the Furious Overfall north of Canada.

1592 and 1599—Wright-Molyneux Globe and map of the world, which Hudson used in searching for the Northwest Passage.

1607—Henry Hudson is hired by the Muscovy Company to find a Northeast Passage to China.

April 9: Henry Hudson leaves England on his first voyage aboard the *Hopewell.*

September 5: Hudson and his crew return to England without finding the Northeast Passage.

1608—*April 22:* Hudson leaves, again on the *Hopewell,* to search the Arctic waters for the Northeast Passage.

August 7: Entry in Hudson's journal that indicates a possible mutiny had been resolved.

August 26: The *Hopewell* returns to England, once again having encountered impassable ice and no Northeast Passage.

September–October: Unable to raise money for a third voyage, Hudson travels to Holland to meet with the directors of the Dutch East India Company.

1609—*January 8:* Hudson signs a contract to look for a Northeast Passage with the Dutch East India Company.

March 25: Hudson and sixteen crew members, English and Dutch, sail north on the *Half Moon,* quickly encountering severe ice.

May 19: Surviving a possible mutiny, Hudson changes directions and sails south and west.

July 3: Hudson and his crew reach Newfoundland.

September 3: The *Half Moon* sails past the south coast of Staten Island and its crew spots the opening to three large rivers.

September 6: First trouble with American Indians. John Coleman, crew member, is killed by an Indian attack.

September 11: The *Half Moon* begins its trip up the Hudson River, which Hudson hopes will become a Northwest Passage.

October 4: Hudson leaves the Hudson River and begins to head toward England; He has not found the Northwest Passage but believes it still exists.

November 7: Hudson and his crew arrive in England and he and the English crew members are put on virtual house arrest; They are forbidden to travel to Holland or to ever work for a foreign country again.

1610—*April 7:* Having convinced a group of wealthy merchants to fund him in a search for the Northwest Passage, Hudson leaves England on the *Discovery* with twenty-two crew members.

November 1: Having searched in vain for the passage, Hudson and his crew begin a cold and hungry winter on the shore of ice-clogged James Bay.

1611—*June 21:* A mutiny, headed by Henry Greene, Robert Juet, and William Wilson surprises Hudson; He, his son, and seven ill and loyal crew members are set adrift in the shallop in James Bay; They are never seen again.

July 28: Four mutineers are killed by Inuits; Juet soon dies of starvation.

October: After a miserable trip across the Atlantic, the blood-soaked *Discovery* limps into England with the remaining mutineers, who would never be punished for their treatment of Hudson and fellow crew members.

Chapter Notes

Chapter 1. Up a Wide, Wide River

1. Donald S. Johnson, *Charting the Sea of Darkness* (Camden, Maine: International Marine, A Division of McGraw-Hill, Inc., 1993), p. 115.

2. Ibid., p. 116.

Chapter 2. Who Was Henry Hudson?

1. Philip Vail, *The Magnificent Adventures of Henry Hudson* (New York: Dodd Mead & Company, 1965), pp. 1–10.

Chapter 3. The World of Henry Hudson

1. Samuel Purchas, *Henry Hudson's Voyages, from Purchas, His Pilgrims, Facsimile Edition* (Ann Arbor, Mich.: University Microfilms, Inc., 1946), Part Three.

2. Donald S. Johnson, *Charting the Sea of Darkness* (Camden, Maine: International Marine, A Division of McGraw-Hill, Inc., 1993), p. 200.

3. Ibid., p. ix.

4. Ibid., p. 4.

5. Llewelyn Powys, *Henry Hudson* (New York: Harper & Brothers Publishers, 1928), p. 5.

6. Johnson, p. 10.

7. Powys, p. 6.

8. Johnson, p. 13.

9. Powys, p. 7.

10. Johnson, p. 20.

11. Powys, p. 15.

12. "Full Text of Robert Juet's Journal," *Long Island Our Story,* n.d.,<http://www.lihistory.com/vault/hs21alv.htm> (May 14, 2001).

13. Johnson, p. 18.

Chapter 4. Is It Really Warm at the North Pole?

1. Philip Vail, *The Magnificent Adventures of Henry Hudson* (New York: Dodd Mead & Company, 1965), p. 18.

2. Llewelyn Powys, *Henry Hudson* (New York: Harper & Brothers Publishers, 1928), p. 26.

3. Ibid., p. 27.

4. Ibid., p. 28.

5. Donald S. Johnson, *Charting the Sea of Darkness* (Camden, Maine: International Marine, A Division of McGraw-Hill, Inc., 1993), p. 27.

6. Powys, p. 29.

7. Ibid.

8. Ibid.

9. Johnson, p. 33.

10. Powys, p. 31.

11. Johnson, p. 36.

12. Ibid.

13. Powys, p. 35.

14. Johnson, p. 41.

15. Ibid.

16. Ibid., p. 45.

Chapter 5. Whales and Walrus Beware!

1. Llewelyn Powys, *Henry Hudson* (New York: Harper & Brothers Publishers, 1928), p. 45.

2. Donald S. Johnson, *Charting the Sea of Darkness* (Camden, Maine: International Marine, A Division of McGraw-Hill, Inc., 1993), p. 56.

3. Ibid., p. 60.

4. Richard Whitbourne, "Newfoundland Mermaid, 1610," *Eyewitness to History,* ed. John Carey (New York: Avon Books, 1987), pp. 165–166.

5. Powys, p. 47.

6. Johnson, p. 69.

7. Ibid., p. 72.

8. Ibid.

Chapter 6. The Dutch East India Company to the Rescue

1. Llewelyn Powys, *Henry Hudson* (New York: Harper & Brothers Publishers, 1928), p. 61.

2. Ibid., p. 72.

3. Donald S. Johnson, *Charting the Sea of Darkness* (Camden, Maine: International Marine, A Division of McGraw-Hill, Inc., 1993), p. 137.

4. Ibid., p. 86.

5. Ibid., p. 87.

Chapter 7. Westward Ho!

1. Donald S. Johnson, *Charting the Sea of Darkness* (Camden, Maine: International Marine, A Division of McGraw-Hill, Inc., 1993), p. 90.

2. Llewelyn Powys, *Henry Hudson* (New York: Harper & Brothers Publishers, 1928), p. 85.

3. Johnson, p. 128.

4. Ibid., p. 129.

5. Ibid.

6. Powys, p. 88.

7. Noel Rae, ed., *Witnessing America: The Library of Congress Book of Firsthand Accounts of Life in America 1600–1900* (New York: A Stonesong Press Book, 1996), pp. 5–6.

8. Johnson, p. 103.

9. Powys, p. 92.

10. "Instructions for the Virginia Colony (1606)," *Henry Hudson: an Englishman in Dutch Service,* 1997, <http://odur.let.rug.nl/~usa/D/1601-1650/virginia/instru.htm> (May 14, 2001).

11. Rae, p. 94; Johnson, p. 130.

12. Johnson, p. 111.

13. Powys, pp. 94–95.

Chapter 8. Feathers and Furs

1. Donald S. Johnson, *Charting the Sea of Darkness* (Camden, Maine: International Marine, A Division of McGraw-Hill, Inc., 1993), p. 116.

2. E. M. Ruttenber, *Indian Tribes of Hudson's River to 1700* (Saugerties, N.Y.: Hope Farm Press, 1998), p. 34. [First published by author in 1872.]

3. Ibid., pp. 34–35.

4. Johnson, p. 117.

5. "Full Text of Robert Juet's Journal," *Long Island Our Story,* n.d.,<http://www.lihistory.com/vault/hs21alv.htm> (May 14, 2001).

6. Powys, p. 96.

7. Johnson, p. 120.

8. Ibid., p. 121.

9. Ibid.

10. Ibid., p. 122.

Chapter 9. The Last Voyage

1. Llewelyn Powys, *Henry Hudson* (New York: Harper & Brothers Publishers, 1928), p. 117.

2. Donald S. Johnson, *Charting the Sea of Darkness* (Camden, Maine: International Marine, A Division of McGraw-Hill, Inc., 1993), p. 131.

3. Powys, p. 118.

4. Ibid.

5. Johnson, p. 207.

6. Ibid., p. 209.

7. Powys, p. 125.

8. Ibid., p. 129.

9. Ibid., p. 136.

10. Johnson, p. 160.

11. Ibid.

12. Ibid., p. 161.

13. Ibid., p. 190.

14. Powys, p. 145.

Chapter 10. Mutiny in a Winter Wonderland

1. Llewelyn Powys, *Henry Hudson* (New York: Harper & Brothers Publishers, 1928), p. 147.

2. Donald S. Johnson, *Charting the Sea of Darkness* (Camden, Maine: International Marine, A Division of McGraw-Hill, Inc., 1993), p. 171.

3. Powys, p. 155.

4. Johnson, p. 172.

5. Ibid., p. 173.

6. Ibid., p. 195.

7. Ibid., p. 174.

8. Ibid.

9. Ibid., p. 179.

10. Ibid.

11. Powys, p. 170.

12. Ibid., p. 175.

13. Johnson, p. 199.

14. Ibid., p. 201.

Chapter 11. The Legacy

1. Llewelyn Powys, *Henry Hudson* (New York: Harper & Brothers Publishers, 1928), p. 188.

2. Philip Vail, *The Magnificent Adventures of Henry Hudson* (New York: Dodd Mead & Company, 1965), pp. 214–217.

3. New Netherland Museum, "Henry Hudson's 1609 Voyage," *Half Moon History,* n.d., <http://www.newnetherland.org/history.htm> (May 14, 2001).

4. Bernard C. Weber, *The Discoverers: An Encyclopedia of Explorers and Exploration* (New York: McGraw-Hill, Inc., 1980), pp. 65–66.

5. Donald S. Johnson, *Charting the Sea of Darkness* (Camden, Maine: International Marine, A Division of McGraw-Hill, Inc., 1993), p. 220.

Further Reading

Goodman, Joan Elizabeth. *Beyond the Sea of Ice: The Voyages of Henry Hudson.* New York: Mikaya Press, 1999.

Santella, Andrew. *Henry Hudson.* Danbury, Conn.: Franklin Watts Incorporated, 2001.

Syme, Ronald. *Henry Hudson.* Tarrytown, N.Y.: Marshall Cavendish Corporation, 1991.

Weiner, Eric. *The Story of Henry Hudson.* New York: Bantam Doubleday Dell Books for Young Readers, 1991.

Whitcraft, Melissa. *The Hudson River.* Danbury, Conn.: Franklin Watts Incorporated, 2000.

Internet Addresses

"Half Moon." Schooner Man: Schooner and Tall Sailing Ships. August 15, 2001. <http://www.schoonerman. com/halfmoon.htm>.

Ian Chadwick. "The life and times of Henry Hudson, explorer and adventurer." *Henry Hudson.* 1997–2001. <http://www.ianchadwick.com/ hudson/hudson1.html>.

PBS Kids. "Henry Hudson." *Learning Adventure In Citizenship.* n.d. <http://www.pbs.org/wnet/newyork/ laic/episode1/topic1/e1_t1_s1-hh.html>.

Index